D0392306

Comrade Chikatilo

THE PSYCHOPATHOLOGY OF RUSSIA'S NOTORIOUS SERIAL KILLER

BY MIKHAIL KRIVICH
AND OL'GERT OL'GIN

Translated by Todd P. Bludeau
Edited by Sandi Gelles-Cole

BARRICADE BOOKS INC.
Fort Lee, New Jersey

Published by BARRICADE BOOKS INC.
1530 Palisade Avenue, Fort Lee, NJ 07024

Distributed by Publishers Group West
4065 Hollis, Emeryville, CA 94608

Published simultaneously in Russia by Text Publishers, Ltd.

Printed in the United States of America.

Library of Congress Cataloging-in-Publication Data

Krivich, Mikhail
    Comrade Chikatilo: the psychopathology of Russia's noto-
rious serial killer/by Mikhail Krivich and Ol'gert Ol'gin.
    p.   cm.
    Translated from the Russian by Todd P. Bludeau
    Edited by Sandi Gelles-Cole
    ISBN 0-942637-90-9 $20.00
    1. Serial muderers—Russia (Federation)—Rostovskaia oblast
—Case studies. 2. Sex crimes—Russia (Federation)—Rostovskaia
oblast—Case studies. 3. Chikatilo, Andrie. 4. Murderers—
Russia (Federation)—Rostovskaia oblast—Biography. 5. Insane,
Criminal and dangerous—Russia (Federation)—Rostovskaia
oblast—Biography. I. Ol'gin, Ol'gert. II. Title.
HV6535.R942R675   1993   92-42104
364.1'523'094777—dc20   CIP

0 9 8 7 6 5 4 3 2 1

Contents

3

Acknowledgements

THE IDEA for writing a book on the so-called "Rostov case" first came to us in June of 1992. We set to work on it at the end of July, finished the rough draft by September and put the final touches to it in the middle of October. We still cannot believe that we were able to accomplish so much over such a short period.

The metaphor that kept us going was that of a regatta. We wanted to be first at the finish line with our book on the shocking history that led to Russia's first open trial of a mass murderer. At the same time, though, we were afraid that our boat would capsize from the overload of facts, statements, interviews and documents we had managed to accumulate. As we navigated our way through them, we had to throw down our oars at times in order to contemplate on the circumstances of the case and to catch our breath from the wave of disgusting and sordid details washing over us. Once the initial revulsion had passed, we were able to forge ahead once again.

Strictly speaking, we had no choice but to hurry. Other factors notwithstanding, it would have been impossible to write about such horrible events at a leisurely pace.

We were taught in school that haste makes waste. We might have won the race, but at what cost? If the reader finds that our book has omitted something or garbled the facts, or that it falls short of his or her expectations, then the blame is ours and ours only. We beg the reader's indulgence.

Having become rather well-versed in the terminology of the criminal code during the writing of this book, the authors would like to make an uncoerced and openhearted confession: we would never have been able to complete this job on our own. Friends, whom we have known and trusted for a long time, as well as total strangers continually gave us their assistance.

We would like to express our gratitude first and foremost to those people who were unsparing of their time and unstinting in sharing with us their recollections, observations, and thoughts. Since we believe that everyone should have the same chances in a race, we did not ask them for exclusive rights to their information. We were just happy that they spoke to us as friends, with candor and understanding.

Our thanks go to Viktor Burakov, Aleksandr Bukhanovsky, Dmitri Veltishchev, Anatoly Yevseyev, Aleksandr Zanosovsky, Vladimir Kazakov, Vladimir Kolesnikov, Issa Kostoyev, Igor Rybakov, Irina Stadnichenko, Marat Khabibulin, Yelena Khramova,

Amurkhan Yandiev and all the others whom we mentioned, or neglected to mention, in our book.

We are grateful to our colleagues from the press who shared their impressions, facts and observations with us.

We are grateful to Lynn Franklin who, with her customary energy, kept pushing us on to the point where suddenly we realized there was no turning back.

We especially thank our translator, Todd Bludeau, who worked night and day to produce this English language translation in record time. We are also grateful to Sandi Gelles-Cole who initiated us in the concept of true crime literature, and who worked with Todd Bludeau on editing and polishing the translation.

Thanks to attorney Mark Kogan, who has been waging his own battle for so many years against the ignorance of our judicial system.

We thank our friends from the Russian publishing house, Text, and especially Vitaly Babenko, who expended a tremendous amount of effort to ensure the book's completion. We are grateful to Andrei Gavrilov and David Feldman for their invaluable assistance in gathering the necessary documents in Moscow and Rostov. We are especially grateful to Yulia Zvarich, who spent her evenings reading the unfinished manuscript and the following mornings pointing out to us the mistakes and errors.

We also extend our thanks to Anna Guseva, Natalia and Olga Guva, Pavel Yevsiukov, Gennady Zakirov, Vadim Kaplun, Alfia Kashafutdinova, Vera Malysheva, Eduard Mikhlin and all our colleagues at Text who prepared this book for publication so quickly.

July-October 1992

A True Crime Story

EVERYTHING that you are about to read, if the horror of it does not repel you, is the absolute truth. All details were taken directly from the actual criminal case and trial proceedings of Andrei Chikatilo, a man accused of fifty-three savage and sadistic murders.

The story told here unfolded in our day and age in the southern Russian city of Rostov-on-Don and its environs: on quiet and noisy streets, in parks and cemeteries, in forests, in vacant lots and on beaches, but most of all in forest belts—barriers of trees and shrubs—situated alongside roads and railroad tracks.

The "true crime" drama has become a popular genre in our country, as popular as detective novels.

This genre has its guidelines. For example, the facts, no matter how terrible they may be, must be scrupulously adhered to; the motives behind the crime, as well as the psychology of both victim and criminal, must be studied. Step by step the chronicle should lead the reader from conception to bloody execution.

That was our plan too, but it didn't quite turn out that way. If this story were to be told step by step, from conception to execution, we would have needed at least thirty pages for each murder and still more for background, investigation and trial. The result would have been a series of books the size of the Encyclopedia Britannica.

Unlike most "true crime" stories, this one is not about one heinous deed, or five or even ten. The actual indictment reads fifty-three, but no one knows how many more there may be. This series of bloody killings took place over twelve years. At the trial there were many witnesses, but not a single eyewitness. And not one victim escaped alive.

We have tried to get all the facts on paper. We can't possibly include everything for one simple reason—not everything is known yet.

Mikhail Krivich
Olgert Olgin

PART I

No Witnesses

No Witness

CHAPTER 1

Hunting For Tongue

THE MID-1980s

A COMMUTER TRAIN has just pulled out of the suburban station in the direction of Rostov-on-Don, after
depositing a dozen or so people on the platform. It is
an in-between time of day: too early to quit work by
an hour or two, but already too late to run errands or
go shopping in the city.

Two people, their backs to the departing train,
walk along the platform together. One is a grown
man about forty years old, maybe a bit older, in a
respectable dark suit and tie. He looks like a func-
tionary. In his left hand he holds a brown, somewhat
worn, briefcase—crammed full, one has to assume,
with important papers from work. To his right, trying
to keep pace with him, is a boy about eleven years
old, dressed in cheap blue jeans of local origin, and a
short-sleeved checkered shirt.

They could be father and son. The boy does not
come up to the man's shoulder in height so he has to
look up when talking to him. The man nods his head
in agreement, looks at his watch and quickens his

13

pace. He arrives first at the stairs leading from the platform to the paths below. The boy follows.

The platform is already empty. The commuters waiting for their train on the opposite side watch the father and son with an indifferent glance and then forget them as soon as they disappear from view.

It is a warm day, near the end of summer. Light clouds float in the sky; a slight breeze wafts the smell of trees and dry grass. The sun peeks out in the blue gaps between the clouds.

The man and boy are arguing about something. It seems they're trying to choose a short cut. They walk side by side along the ties, then cross over to a well-worn path between the railroad embankment and a patch of woods to the right. Here the path is narrow, so the man steps out first as if showing the way. Finally he stops and waves his arm—time to turn off. They both disappear among the trees.

One of them vanishes forever.

* * *

About thirty years ago trees began to be planted in this bare edge of steppe alongside the railroad and highway as a defense against the steppe's winds and dust storms. In addition to comforting the traveler's gaze, the trees also keep fires away from the fields and villages. Maples, lindens, elms and rowans sprouted, stretched their limbs, gave birth to new shoots and sheltered in their shade both grass and bush. By now, the plantings have grown into a small forest cutting a swath along the embankment thirty steps wide.

This wooded area is known in Russian as a *lesopolosa*, or "shelterbelt." Here it is cool and damp, as in a real forest, and smells of fallen leaves and mushrooms. In just a few days the mushroom hunters will arrive. For these dwellers of the steppe, unspoiled by the abundance of the forests to the north, this strip of trees is a gift.

The path is narrow and seldom used. The man allows the boy to walk ahead, pushing the branches of bushes out of the way to avoid getting struck in the face. He turns around and looks questioningly at the man who nods his head: *We're going the right way*. Only a few steps separate them. The man quickens his pace slightly and fastens his eyes on the faded jeans hugging the boy's lean bottom.

The boy again turns and asks something—*Don't we have to turn soon to get back onto the road?* But the man acts as if he hasn't heard. He is practically right next to him, the distance of an outstretched arm. His face is covered in sweat, his eyes are glassy, and his jaw hangs open.

In the train, he appeared to be calm and sober-minded, perhaps a bit boring. That's often the way grownups seem. He had spoken quietly, inquiring where the boy had come from and where he was headed. He asked if he was hungry. He told him about his *dacha*, or country house, and invited the boy to stop by for a bite to eat and to pick fruit in his garden before they headed back together to the station.

It's the end of the day—no need to be in a hurry to get anywhere. Again the man asks questions, showing an interest in what the boy reads and recommending books to borrow from the library. A normal guy, or so he appears. . .

Suddenly there is nothing at all normal in his glassy eyes. He seems to peer out from hell, just like in a horror film when the face on the screen becomes twisted in a terrible grimace.

Perhaps this vision even flashes through the boy's mind for a fleeting moment, but he doesn't have time to comprehend that all this is truly happening to him, that a sinewy arm with a huge grasping paw is coming toward him, seizing him by the shoulder, tearing his shirt, and then throwing him onto the ground into the bushes, the branches whipping his face. The boy falls on his back, and is dragged along the clearing between the hazel grove, overgrown with coarse grass. He feels a heavy, foul-smelling body on top of him. Fear has deprived him of the strength to cry out. He cannot understand why stiff fingers are furiously ripping the fly on his jeans and stripping off his clothes. It is as if he were caught in a bear trap. Still, at a certain moment when he becomes conscious of the fact that this is not a dream, he manages to find the strength to tear away, slipping out from under the iron grip, jump up and scream for help.

But there is not a soul around, and his screams are absorbed by the trees, who watch in silence.

A hard fist knocks the wind out of him. The boy doubles over, gasping in pain, as another smashing blow sends him crashing to the ground. The man, huge, frenzied, his pants down at his ankles, genitals exposed and dangling, binds the boy's arms with cord and shoves him face down onto the wet grass. He crawls all over the boy, the weight of his 220 pounds pressing him down, breathing hoarsely, thrusting his iron fingers into his behind, kneading, squeezing and tearing.

The boy attempts to crawl out from under him, screaming, but his assailant suddenly pulls out a knife and slashes the boy's neck with the blade.

The pain doesn't come right away—just a new wave of icy fear and revulsion. The boy feels hot rivulets of blood on his neck and a vile dampness on his loins, against which the man's sweaty body is still pressing.

The boy cries out hoarsely, but the man, coiling himself around him, clamps the boy's mouth shut with his palm, stuffs some earth and leaves between his teeth, seizes his neck with his huge paws, and begins choking him.

The boy is still alive when the man rises from his body and rolls the bloody mass over, face up toward him. Forcing open the boy's dirt- and blood-smeared lips, he brings the young face up to his own and sinks his teeth into the boy's tongue. He bites off a piece and swallows.

The sinewy half-naked man sprawls alongside his victim, panting heavily, from time to time opening his bloodied mouth into a deep yawn. The boy's body is convulsing, and he groans. To silence him, the man gets halfway up, grabs the knife laying nearby, and strikes hard. Once, twice, three times. In the neck, chest, stomach, lower and lower. Ten, twenty, thirty times. . .

Long after the boy is silent the man keeps hacking away. He stabs in a monotonous rhythm, with his left hand, bringing himself closer and closer to his lifeless victim. At times he hastens the blows, not even bothering now to remove the knife but moving it back and forth in the same place. He stretches himself out on the still warm corpse, and suddenly the man's body stiffens and trembles in orgasm. When he has calmed down, he raises himself to his knees and begins dully and methodically cutting the clothing and the body—from top to bottom, right to left. With one abrupt motion, one blow, he lops off the boy's tongue and, squeezing the bloody lump in his fist, begins running war whoops around the corpse.

"I'm a Red partisan!" cries the man, holding onto his slipping pants. "I took his tongue! I captured the enemy! I'm a Red partisan!"

Then he grows silent, becomes all business-like. With a dexterity acquired from habit, he removes the clumps of clothing from the body, unties the cord which has bound the boy's hands, and wraps it around the balled-up rags. He stands, wipes himself off, and pulls on his pants. He glances at the blood-drenched body and at his own hands, sees blood on

the palms, and fastidiously uses the rags to wipe
them off. Then, using his feet to rake dead leaves
closer to the body, he begins to cover it. It is at that
moment that he notices a cheap watch on the boy's
wrist. He bends over, undoes the strap, sticks the
watch in his pocket, and continues throwing leaves
on the body.

In a week's time the mushroom hunters will
stumble upon the corpse.

The man's agitation has almost subsided.
Grabbing the bundle of clothing and his briefcase, he
heads toward the station along the same path. At the
edge of the woods, he chucks the bundle into a ditch
by the road.

Detectives will find the clothing.

An hour-and-a-half after the two had entered the
woods, the grown man in a dark suit and tie, with a
brown briefcase in his hand, emerges and walks
toward the suburban station to meet the commuter
train.

CHAPTER 2

The Man From Hell

SUMMER 1992

DURING THE YEARS of Soviet power the courts fell into a state of impoverishment and dilapidation: both the court as process and the court as building. When the blindfold was removed from the Russian Minerva's eyes in 1917, at the same time as her scales for weighing good and evil were requisitioned by the Bolsheviks, the goddess of justice, blinded by the bloody dawn of the new era, began mowing down victims left and right.

No special environment was especially necessary for this. The court, except in the most unusual circumstances, was transformed from an esteemed, respectable, even majestic, institution into a second-rate department, on a par with the wash-house.

To this day Russian judges huddle, for the most part, in seedy buildings, unsuited for courtroom activities. The ceilings leak, the masonry is peeling from the walls, it is freezing in winter, and stifling in summer. The judicial employees, who enjoy neither the people's respect (though it is supposedly the people's court) nor a decent salary, at times threaten to strike, or at times ceases to work altogether due to the utter impossibility of continuing in such circumstances.

In fact, an extraordinary conference was convened in Moscow in June 1992 by magistrates from the Moscow region. For half a day they debated whether to announce a partial strike and simply quit hearing criminal cases. They were driven to this rash action by their miserable salary and lousy conditions. Finally the minister of justice personally intervened to dissuade the judges from making such a desperate gesture. This time he succeeded.

Only recently has there been any hope for improvement. It was thought that, with the departure of the communists from the scene, the best buildings in the cities and villages might be vacated. These included private residences belonging to the former district committees and regional committees, various domiciles of political enlightenment, and Party educational institutions where orthodox students were pumped full with Marxist-Leninist theory. These buildings were to be handed over to those who needed them the most—children and the courts. Nonetheless, the judges still preside today where they presided before. Across the entire country, from the capital to the provinces, courtroom proceedings are carried out in cramped and uncomfortable quarters, just as they were during Gorbachev's, Brezhnev's, Khrushchev's and Stalin's days.

The Rostov Provincial Court is an exception. A sturdy two-story private house built during czarist times, it features an awninged main entrance, high ceilings, columns and stuccoed molding on the facade. It is painted yellow, the official and traditional color of Russian bureaucracy, and sits prestigiously on Socialist Street, a quiet, attractive tree-lined thoroughfare despite its name. The court is just a few steps away from the main artery in Rostov, until recently called Engels Street but nowadays renamed, as in olden times, Bolshaya Sadovaya, even though signs bearing the name of the proletariat-loving German capitalist have yet to be removed.

The building in which the Rostov Court is located is called the House of Justice. When compared to other, lower-ranked courts, it could properly be called a Palace of Justice, for it is spacious inside. Polite militiamen keep the peace. Ladies of the court, many among them attractive and well-dressed, scurry about in the vestibule. Even the visitors, who normally in Russian courts look like pitiful lost souls, here look cleaner and more presentable.

This court normally hears appeals or cases of special importance. The case being heard on the first floor, in the largest room of the institution, Courtroom Number 5, is unusual not only for Rostov, but for the whole world. It is a very rare occurrence when the news coming out of the Rostov Court gets reported in newspapers and telecasts around the world?

The session begins at ten a.m. sharp. For a few minutes beforehand, several women, clutching shopping bags in their hands, are already standing outside the high oak door that leads inside. From all appearances the bags are full, meaning that the women have been up since dawn making the rounds of the shops, buying up whatever products are available. Everyone knows it is necessary to get up early to go shopping before everything disappears from the shelves, for if it is postponed until later, when the court is in recess, a family can risk going hungry.

In the hall, halfway from the entrance, an old woman in worn house slippers has lain a wooden tray with white buns. There is no line, but little by little the buns are snapped up by the militiamen, the visitors, and the courtroom ladies. Some are chewing, others are tucking them away for later. The women near the door are also buying and putting the buns in their bottomless bags: they'll come in handy.

An electronic screen, similar to the ones in train stations that give information on arriving and departing trains, is supposed to provide information concerning in which rooms the various civil and criminal cases are being heard on any given day—except that no matter which button is pushed, no answer will be given; the machine is broken. As compensation for this inconvenience, one can read in the screen's center the following exhortation: "Strictly and conscientiously observe the laws of Soviet power. V.I. Lenin." Either the workers forgot to remove it, or they're in no hurry to do so—as though there still remains the chance that life will suddenly turn upside down, and once again the long-suffering Russian people will have to live according to the precepts of Lenin.

The door is flung open, and the court secretary, a lanky young woman, motions everyone in. "Families of the victims first," warns a militiaman. The women with their bags—these are the families of the victims—surge forward. They are followed by the others, maybe ten people in all, no more.

The courtroom is spacious, a fitting site for a major trial of global notoriety. There is seating for at least two hundred fifty arrayed under three massive chandeliers and high lancet windows receding toward the ceiling.

The wooden benches have been chiseled into by more than one generation of habitues who have recorded for posterity their names, dates, little arrow-pierced hearts, and naive obscenities. It is an attribute of public places, be it a waiting hall in a bus or train station or a university auditorium, that is touching to the Russian soul. While absorbed in reading this folklore, a person can forget where he is.

But he has only to raise his head for everything to fall immediately into place: a massive bench sits under the windows, with three armchairs behind it. The middle one rises a bit higher than the other two and is adorned with the coat of arms of the former Soviet Russia—a hammer and sickle and ears of corn wound about by a ribbon. This has already been officially replaced with the two-headed (though crownless) eagle, but here it has been touched, just like the Leninist quotation. The carving on the backs of the other chairs is simpler—just a hammer and sickle.

Those public gathered in this courtroom is not paying attention to the armchairs and their symbols. Their gaze is directed toward an iron cage, painted a light beige, that stands alongside the right wall behind a low barrier with carved white balusters. The cage looks homemade, as if slapped together by a skilled metalworker out of improvised materials. The top is covered with a rather thick metal netting. Inside is a simple bench. A staircase, communicating with the heavily padlocked and grated door of the cage, goes down, beyond the barrier. Where, exactly, it leads cannot be made out from the room.

Militiamen, along with several strapping soldiers from the internal troops appear decked out in peaked caps with crimson bands, appear. These are strong lads, specially chosen, with barrel-like chests that drip with medals attesting to their athletic prowess successes and military training. One of them opens the lock, enters the cage and carefully inspects it: a fixed look on the bench, a fixed look under the bench.

Suddenly, harking to an inaudible command, the militiamen and soldiers line up along the barrier, screening the defendant from the stares of the curious. Nonetheless, in the gaps between the balusters, three heads can be seen emerging from below. Two are in uniformed caps; the third, between them, is uncovered, grayish-white. The heads appear unex-

pectedly and maliciously, as if rising up from the
nether regions. Instantly they separate. The soldiers
push the stooped, gray-haired person into the cage,
slam the door and click the lock shut.

The defendant, Andrei Chikatilo, has taken his
place. A cordon forms around the cage.

Up until this moment, it has been calm in the
courtroom. The women have been conversing among
themselves in hushed tones on the benches reserved
for the aggrieved; the warrant officer has been quietly
instructing his subordinates; the technicians have
been setting up video cameras, and the court secretary has been running back and forth from the conference room with papers. The noise level is about the
same as at a matinee screening in a movie theater
before the lights are turned off.

But as soon as the gray head of the man from hell
appears between the powerful shoulders of his
escorts and is placed behind bars, a piercing feminine
shriek emanates from the benches for the families of
the victims.

"Son of a bitch! Scoundrel, *pi-da-ras!*"

The man in the cage sits bent, practically in two,
his face turned away from the room. His gray head is
still.

"Cannibal! Filthy pig! You're not worth shit!"
shouts a gaunt middle-aged woman with dirty blond
hair neatly pinned up in a bun. "I'll kill your wife,
your children, all of them!"

The woman's voice grows calmer. She has stopped shouting, appearing to be taking measure of the man behind the bars.

"Sure, you sit there, smiling. But what was it like for our children?"

The man in the cage doesn't move an inch. The other women sitting next to the distraught woman nod their heads in agreement.

"How could you? You're in your fifties. Grandchildren. . ." Her tone is level. It sounds as if she is mildly rebuking an acquaintance who has uttered words unbecoming to old age. Then suddenly she explodes again:

"You scoundrel! Sadist! *Pidaras!* Jew son of a bitch!"

She knows, of course, that the defendant is no Jew at all, that he is pure Slav, a "Ukie," but with a lexicon lacking in curses she spits in his face all the insulting words she knows from childhood, and in Russia from time immemorial "Jew," "Jewish mug," and similarly related phrases have always enjoyed privileged status among expletives.

Chikatilo stares at the floor indifferently. From time to time he rocks back and forth, as if in prayer, and yawns—the veins can be seen rippling under his carefully shaven skin. The soldiers posted by the cage glance at the woman and smile. Sympathetically.

She screams for a few minutes and then begins to tire. The scene is becoming drawn out and already seems unbearable when the secretary, cutting her short, calls out into the courtroom:

"All rise! Court is now in session!"

Silence. Everyone stands.

The judges' gowns and caps are like the ones seen in foreign movies and, until recently, in Moscow's Constitutional Court. Three men of medium height, dressed in dark suits as befits the occasion, move down the aisle like a chain. Each carries in his arms several bulging, heavy, already slightly worn, folders in red and blue cardboard bindings—the volumes of the criminal case. The judge, Leonid Borisovich Akubzhanov, is the first to occupy his seat at the table, under the antiquated coat of arms. His helpers, who are called "assessors," sit in the armchairs with the hammers and sickles. This trial has no jury.

The head of the guard removes the cordon from the cage, leaving two armed sentries to stand watch. They are posted on either side, their eyes fixed constantly on the defendant. Every half hour the guard will be changed with picture-perfect precision.

The defense attorney and the prosecutor take their places behind tables set up in front of the cage. The judge declares that court is in session, and immediately is faced with a procedural snag. The three men, clutching red and white folders, retire to the conference room.

Hardly have the three dark suits disappeared into the judge's sanctuary when a familiar voice cries out:

"*Pidaras!* Filthy pig! My husband goes off to work clean and returns clean. Doesn't carry any knives in his briefcase. Your wife, you vulture, knew everything, everything."

The woman's name is Polina Dmitrievna Ishutina. She lives far from here, outside Bryansk. Her twenty-year-old daughter from her first marriage, Anna Lemesheva, was murdered July 19, 1984.

In the indictment handed down, Anna's death is numbered as episode 30. But she isn't the thirtieth victim. The first five counts of the indictment are only for corruption of minors, meaning that she is the twenty-fifth murder victim.

Whenever there is any pause or interruption in the court ritual, Polina Dmitrievna hurls her accusations. Time has not healed her sorrow. Before the court sits the alleged—for her, the obvious—perpetrator of a terrible loss. She pours out her grief and incurable hatred toward this person in threats and curses.

She screams. Her lamentations fill the blank spaces in the trial. Half-an-hour later, no one will even notice.

The judge and the assessors return to their places. It is time for examination of the victims' relatives to begin. The first witness to take the stand is Polina Dmitrievna.

The judge says softly that she can give her testimony sitting if it is too much a burden to stand, but Polina Dmitrievna, with a heavy gait, steps up to the judges' bench, signs a piece of paper about taking responsibility for giving false evidence—which since 1917 in Russia has replaced the practice of swearing upon the Bible—and returns to the witness box.

Yes, she is Ishutina Polina Dmitrievna, forty-five years old, employed as a school assistant manager. Showing almost no emotion, she tells the court what she had been doing on that horrible summer day in 1984, where she was when she learned of her daughter's disappearance, and how she arrived at police headquarters to identify the body. It had been discovered outside Rostov six days after the murder, in a wooded belt alongside the paths leading from the railroad tracks, not too far from the Kirpichnaya Station near the city of Shakhty.

Numerous knife wounds had been found on Anna's body, delivered to both eyesockets, the left temple, the left thigh—no less than ten—and the area of the lactic glands and pubis. The last ones were made after she was already dead. When Anna had died, and the murderer had received his sexual satisfaction by wiggling around on top of his bloodied and dying prey, he undressed the victim completely, cut up and shredded her clothing, cut off both nipples, butchered her sexual organs and cut out her uterus.

This is drily and succinctly stated in the materials of the criminal case: "[He] bit off and swallowed the nipples of the lactic glands. Avenging his impotence, he cut out the sexual organs, then threw them out, but gnawed the uterus."

Anna had been on her way home after a visit to the dentist at a local clinic. A tooth was aching under the crown. He had tempted her into the woods on that hot day, asking her to go for a swim in a pond. She'd turned out to be stronger than he had imagined, and only after striking her a few times with his knife was he able to take control. He used a basic carpenter's knife with a plastic handle.

Polina Dmitrievna Ishutina relates all this practically without emotion, answering the questions haltingly. It is only when the judge, delicately choosing his words and trying not to cause any more pain, asks her: "What kind of girl was she?" is her stoic demeanor shattered.

Choking and sobbing, she says, "A good girl, never harmed anyone. . ."

A medic in a white gown brings her a glass of water.

Two medics are constantly on duty in the room. For some reason they sit with their backs to the public, facing the judges' bench, as if the judges might require aid. They turn, however, when they hear the sobbing.

The judge asks the final, formal question:

"What else can you add to the nature of the case?"

Ishutina pushes away the glass of water, throws her head back and screams horribly:

"So, cannibal, did you eat your fill of our children's flesh? Let me at him! Let me!" And to the judge, imploringly: "Please, give him to me. I'll cut him up, I'll kill him. Leonid Borisovich, give him to me."

But the accused, the one wanted for revenge, sitting sideways on the bench, turns away from the sufferers as much as he possibly can. His hands, as prison laws require, are restrained behind his back. A man might get used to it after a year and a half in prison. He yawns, opening his mouth wide, as if he has nothing to do with what they're talking about here, as if he is not the one the crowd is demanding to lynch.

In Rostov and nearby, in wooded belts, in thickets of reeds, in vacant lots and cemeteries, he raped, tortured, killed, mocked his victims, dismembered and ate them. The bloody trail led to the Urals and the environs of Moscow, to St. Petersburg and Tashkent, Krasnodar and Zaporozhe. For twelve years he was tracked, but somehow he eluded all the snares laid out for him until one day in 1990 the trap finally slammed shut.

In the course of the investigation, almost as a side effect, 95 other murders, not attributable to him, were discovered, as were 245 other rapes, 140 aggravated assaults and 600 other less serious crimes.

Naturally, mistakes are committed in the course of investigations and during trials. Sometimes the facts get shuffled, or the truth is deliberately obscured. But could it be that the evidence for all fifty-three crimes was false? If Chikatilo could only be charged with one of the murders attributed to him, then he is a creature from hell, a vampire.

Another outstanding fact about this case is that, even though the trial of Andrei Chikatilo could be called the trial of the century—about which so much had been written in the press—in summer of 1992 the court, after a rather long recess, resumed its work before a courtroom that was practically empty. The public consisted of the families of the victims, the witnesses, judge, assessors, secretary, defense lawyer, prosecutor, medics, guards, a youthful employee of the local paper and a hardened reporter from a Moscow paper, three students from the law faculty who were more concerned about their upcoming exams, two sturdy lads developing their muscles by squeezing a tennis ball, an older man snoozing in the last row, and a casual passer-by looking in for a moment before leaving. And that's it!

The local press devoted constant attention to the trial. One would think that the public would break down the doors to get in. No such thing. The same newspapers reported the arrival in Rostov of "'Vampire,' the one and only Russian-Canadian theater of horrors in the world, featuring werewolves, chimeras, monsters, zombies, bloodsuckers and other evil spirits in a superthriller entitled 'Nightmares in Hell.'" This spectacle had no trouble getting an audience. But here was a real living, breathing vampire. What Canadian show could compare with this?

Meanwhile, on a summer day, the testimony of the families of the victims continued in courtroom number five in the Rostov House of Justice. Women, their faces aged from sorrow, relate the worst days of their lives. Each time the judge asks one of them about her dead child, she wails as if the grief is only just settling in.

Their children were of various types: well-groomed and abandoned, healthy and sick, bright and intellectually slow. But they had been alive. At one time they had been alive.

Sipping water and calming herself somewhat, one of the women said, "God help us live through all this. And you too, Your Honor. There's only one thing I'm afraid of, and that's that they will find him (gesturing toward the cage) insane. And he won't be punished." Her shoulders stop quivering, and in a stronger voice, says, "Okay, no one can return our children to us. But nothing can protect him from us. I'll get a gun. . ."

There is a stirring in the room. The militiamen and the soldiers cannot conceal their smiles—what a gutsy thing to say. Because it is so close to the truth. Any one of the women could bring a weapon, even a grenade launcher, into the room. No one is inspected; there are no metal detectors. All one has to do is sit about ten steps from that yawning monster, whip out a shotgun and blow the monster to kingdom come, rather than rely upon justice to do its job.

The judge uses that moment to announce a recess. All rise and watch the judicial troika make their exit, weighed down by the heavy tomes of the case. The doors of the cage open, and two broad-shouldered soldiers drag out the defendant. Squeezed between them, he runs, practically sliding down the stairs before vanishing into hell.

The public walks out into the vestibule to stretch. The families of the victims keep together. Among them are two young girls—apparently on their own. Cartons of eggs are set out on a small table, the same one from which the buns were sold. A few people surround the table to make sure they get their share.

From the room emerges the defense lawyer, Marat Zaidovich Khabibulin. The women cluster around him and talk about the trial in completely calm tones. Their hatred does not spread to him. He's just a court-appointed lawyer doing his job.

The recess is over. The accused is back in his cage, the judges behind their bench. Attorney Khabibulin turns to the judge. His client is prepared to make a statement.

"What do you have there?" the judge asks sharply.

For the first time that day the defendant stands to his full height. He produces from his pocket some scribbled pieces of paper and shoves them through the bars to a militiaman, who in turn hands them over to the judge.

There is a long pause. The judge reads the handwritten pages, and then gives them to the assessors. The defendant, still standing, waits.

"Tell us what you have," the judge finally pronounces.

"It's all written there." His voice is flat and low.

"Your statement has been appended to the case. If you have something to say, don't drag it out. You're on trial, we're taking oral depositions here. So what is it you want to say?"

He stands silently, slightly rocking back and forth. He yawns.

From outside the room someone shouts, "What did you do at night?"

He is silent.

The newspapers have published photographs of him. In one, taken immediately after his arrest, he is a sullen, middle-aged man in glasses, with a rumpled face and hostile little eyes. He looks like a pencil-pusher—perhaps a technician from a provincial design office. In a different photo the defendant sits in his cage on the first day of the trial. His head is shaven, and in his eyes there is a vacuous stare. His arms are excessively long and powerful—the arms of an orangutan. He is wearing a brightly colored shirt with open collar. In this photo he looks like a murderer.

There is still one more photograph, also taken through the bars, but at a later date. In this one he is laughing out loud. It is not clear what it is that has him so amused, but his tiny mouth is bared in a grin, lascivious little eyes are squinty and his sharp chin pressed to his neck.

Today he looks different, though the shirt he wears under a gray sport coat is the same as before. It's a noticeable shirt, adorned with Olympic symbols. Thousands like them were worn during the 1980 Olympic Games in Moscow. Over the years people wore theirs out and then discarded them.

But this fellow is thrifty. He kept his. It was in this very same shirt that he, equipped with a knife and rope, went in search of his last unsuspecting victim. The rope wasn't always needed, he would say. Sometimes the knife alone was enough. Later, in the toilet at work, in an airport or a train station, he painstakingly washed off all the bloody traces in a sink—not so out of fear as out of neatness.

Thrifty and neat.

The gray suit he is wearing is clean and pressed, although it is not one of his own. It has been provided by the prison. True, it is baggy on him. The defendant in general appears to be a tad shrunken, as if the air has been let out of him. He doesn't appear to be very tall.

"He's the same height as me," says Aleksandr Yurievich Germanov, a gentle giant of a man who heads the militia detail. "A year and a half in solitary confinement would take a few inches off anyone."

His hair, grown out after the prison barber had shaved it, is dirty gray. There is a large bald spot on the crown of his head. Foppish sideburns and an unbecoming pointy chin complete the external appearance. All in all there is nothing remarkable about him. Any person who passed him on the street would not have reason to remember him. Not a very pleasant personality, but that is now, while he is in the cage. During the times he roamed the stations, beaches and streets in search of bloody pleasures, he must have seemed pleasant enough, at least to his victims.

When one becomes aware of what he has done, it becomes difficult to look upon him. No one in the room stares at him for long.

"So are you going to speak or not?" the judge asks, irritated.

He begins to talk. Slowly, disjointedly, eyes down. Long pauses.

The judge and everyone in the room wait patiently.

"My head is killing me all the time. . . Dizzy spells, nightmares . . . Rats are following me . . . In the cell . . . I'm being poisoned by radiation. . ."

Delirium? Wait a moment.

"This trial from the very beginning hasn't been conducted right. It's a kind of farce. I wrote to the Prosecutor General. There should be seventy incidents attributed to me. Not fifty-three, but seventy."

The public pricks up its ears. The judge lifts his head.

"But everyone here is in a hurry. . . To me it's all the same—more, less. But why the rush? I signed everything at the inquest, without looking. I assumed responsibility for everything. But now I think that I somehow don't remember six episodes. The time in Zaporozhye I was already on vacation, not on a business trip. . . And I didn't get any crabs from her. . . They told me that if she had them then it must mean that I had them too. But I didn't have them. . . No one wants to hear the truth, they just want to get it over with as quickly as possible. . . All right then, so how long is it going to take?"

The judge is busily writing something. His face is dark and troubled. By what? By the fact that six murders are suddenly put to doubt? Or by the seventeen new ones looming before him, as a result of which the case will have to be submitted to a further inquiry? By the nonsense about rats and radiation? Is the defendant making a calculated attempt to create an insanity defense? That is just the angle the relatives of the victims fear. The man continues in a low voice, mumbling as if to himself:

"The court doesn't want to hear me. But I want to tell them everything about my life, about how I was mocked and humiliated. . .so they'll all know . . . The doctors told me: you're more a woman than a man. You have a woman's waist and breasts. You should have had an operation in childhood to make you a woman. I wasn't considered a man in the army. 'Ukie' they said when they heard my name. And 'old woman.' They grabbed my tits, humiliations like that. . . I fought against the Soviet mafia my whole life. My father was a commander in the partisan forces. . . It's not his fault that he was captured. . . To this day he has not been rehabilitated. . . It's all there in Moscow, in the archives. . . I have to go to Moscow, but how can I do it now? And there's rats running around in the cell, and radiation too. . ."

He lapses into a lengthy silence, as if to allow time for listeners to reflect on his words. To find meaning in his rambling speech. Just what is concealed in this viscous flow of words? In the room, voices are speaking in whisper. One of the relatives of the victims laughs loudly. There is a changing of the guard before the cage, emphasized by the stamping of boots.

"Is that all you have to say?" the judge asks sharply. "Then sit down. We'll get to the bottom of this. Session closed. Recess until tomorrow at ten o'clock."

All rise and follow the judges out with their eyes. Quickly and undetectably, the accused is hustled from his cage. When he reaches the very bottom of the stairs there is the sound of a lock clicking shut.

We will get to the bottom of this, the judge's expression seems to say.

CHAPTER 3

The First Victim Who Could Have Been the Last

DECEMBER 1978

TO FOLLOW IN the killer's footsteps is to walk a path strewn with the mutilated corpses of adults and children. The first step—as far as the investigation knows—was made on the 22nd of December, 1978. The first victim was Lenochka Zakotnova.

That's how she was usually called—by her diminutive name—because she was nine years old.

In retrospect it seems almost incredible that this little girl could have been the first, last, and only victim.

If the killer had been apprehended and exposed— maybe not right away, maybe even half a year after Lenochka's murder—the chain would have been snapped at its first link.

If...

Lenochka Zakotnova was not the only victim. Just the first.

* * *

43

The place is the city of Shakhty, Rostov oblast, 26 Mezhevoy Lane. That much can be read in the indictment.

As can be determined from meteorological data, December 22, 1978 was overcast and cool. The day we authors visited the site of the murder was a cloudless summer day in 1992.

We had traveled to Shakhty from Rostov the same way the girl's murderer had come here hundreds of times before.

The express train from Rostov to Moscow rushes past the city of Shakhty barely before the Rostov passengers have had time to arrange their belongings and settle comfortably in their seats. A suburban commuter train covers the same distance in about fifty minutes, a bus in a little more than an hour.

After deliberating, we chose the bus.

For what sins has Russia been punished with such bus and train stations and airports? Whether in the capitals or the provinces, whether new or old, large or small, they differ only in their degree of pomposity and number of passengers. It makes no difference whether it is Domodedovo Airport in Moscow, a railroad station somewhere in Verkhnaya Salda, Warsaw Station in St. Petersburg, or a bus station in the First of May village of any province of any region. There is always the same pungent, inescapable stench—a mixture of filthy, untended washrooms, cheap perfume, unwashed bodies, chlorine and some indefinable road-type smell. Unhappy old women and haughty

Caucasians, gypsies and little Vietnamese people, children drinking carbonated water and throwing coin after coin into arcade games, an endless stream of lieutenants migrating God knows where with their unattractive and prematurely aged wives and babies in soiled diapers. And scores of travelers on official business crisscrossing the country to buy, sell, exchange or beg metal, lumber, kerosene, sugar and everything else.

Indeed, the suspect accused of murder, yawning in the courtroom, prattling inanities to himself, also hails from this fraternity of suppliers and solicitors. Without them, it seems, the whole shaky system of production, soldered together in slapdash fashion during the long years of Soviet power, would come crashing to the ground. He also spent a good deal of time hanging out in the stations waiting for a train, a bus, or a plane. In his search for victims, he undoubtedly walked up and down between the benches, stepping over handbags, suitcases, and bundles.

The Rostov bus station, as well as the one in Shakhty, was built recently. These stations are a bit cleaner than is usual in Russia, but even so, there is still that same inescapable station scent, the same sickly-sweet lemonade; the same bundles and bags, potties, gray old women in scarves, scraggly cats and dogs; the same confusion in front of the ticket windows, and the same crush of people getting on a bus.

Once on board, there's no air. Arguments frequently break out over the same seat for which two passengers inevitably hold a ticket. The aisle is crammed with belongings, but in an effort to be more economical, gum-cracking kids ranging in age from seven to ten are stuffed in among them.

Kids just like these, with no one watching out for them, were tempted—with gum—by the murderer.

The road to Moscow passes by field after field. The very monotony of the landscape causes drowsiness. Road signs indicate "Red something-or-other." It could be the name of a sovkhoz, kolkhoz, or village. Any map of the Rostov region is littered with names like Red October, Red Don, Red Dawn, Red Crimea, Red Steppe or, simply, Red. How do the natives tell them apart?

The majority of the population in Shakhty is engaged in mining—*shakhty* literally means "mines." Shakhty is young Lenochka's city. It is also the city of her murderer.

At the bus station, where Lenochka's killer often wandered, are the same kinds of careworn, unsmiling people as on the bus. Young boys wear sneakers made in China, pants made in Turkey, and shirts from origins unknown. There are swollen women with varicose veins, leathery men with long sideburns. Dusty refuse pits, polluted water, unhealthy work, bread, lard, potatoes and macaroni.

Next to the station is a wooden booth proclaiming "Gifts of the Forest." A smaller sign says "Kiosk of the Shakhty Forest Preserve. Balsam sold here." The ingredients of the balsam are scribbled out in hand: extract of rosehip, nettles, cinnamon, and citrus plants. Thirty-seven proof.

From a darkened corner of the booth two men appear, intoxicated to a shade of purple. "We've been drinking half a year," one says, "and we still seem to be alive."

Too late to refuse their offer now; the glasses have already been poured. We take a swallow, and our eyes practically pop out of our heads. Our throats burn. We pour out the rest onto the road. The two men look at us in silent disapproval.

At a taxi stand, there are a dozen cars. The drivers stand in a bunch, idly conversing. Upon hearing the address, they repeat it unenthusiastically, "Mezhevoy, did you say?"

They scratch the backs of their heads, exchanging glances. "Isn't that the place where you picked up some brick for your garage last year?"

"Who the hell knows? Maybe there, maybe not..."

Shakhty is not a big city—it is smaller than Rostov. One of the "townies" agrees to take us to Mezhevoy Lane.

This is where it all happened fourteen years ago.

The houses on Mezhevoy Lane are situated close to one another. Little by little the lane narrows and turns into a rutted road squeezed between fences. A car could barely pass here without scratching its sides. The fences here are fashioned from rusted pipes, rotten wood, or iron bedsprings. Poverty can be picturesque, but here it is merely depressing.

Finally we find it: number 26, painted in black and white right on the wall.

A wretched shack sits atop a hillock. It will be mentioned more than once in the two hundred twenty-five volumes of the case. Its former owner calls it a dugout, a half-forgotten word from way back during the war. But it rather accurately describes the small, dirty green shed, haphazardly covered with boards and smeared in places with mud. The windows have soiled and cracked panes. Several wooden steps lead to a bleached, wooden outhouse next to it. Still a bit further to the right, literally a few steps away, stands another, equally dilapidated, little home. A disheveled old woman, hanging clothes outside, casts a mistrustful glance over her shoulder at us.

It almost seems inevitable something hellish had to happen in this setting.

Back then it wasn't summer, but a frigid December day. The narrow, pitted lane was covered with wet and dirty snow. It was along this lane, from the streetcar stop "Grushevsky Bridge" on Soviet Street, that a grown man with a longish nose, accompanied by a girl about ten years old, headed toward the shack, that is, house number 26. The man, according to eyewitnesses, was walking three or four steps ahead.

The investigators have been able to determine with absolute precision what both the suspect and his victim were wearing at the time. The man was clad in a long dark overcoat and beaver lamb cap. He was carrying a bag, out of which wine bottles protruded. The girl was wearing a red coat with a hood trimmed in black fur, a rabbit hat, felt boots, and carrying a schoolbag.

Several days later, when the girl's body was found in the Grushevka, she was dressed in the same clothing.

The man's black coat and brown beaver lamb cap with cloth top would also turn up, though it would take some time—twelve years. When the man was arrested, and a search of his apartment was carried out, many old and worn things would be found, including that same coat and hat. He didn't like to part with things, not even old, useless stuff.

Second-grader Lenochka Zakotnova was an animated little girl. After school she attended dance class. Afterwards, Lenochka and her friends would go home, put on their ice skates and skate awhile. Then they would part. For both Lena and her schoolmates it was just a few minutes' walk to home.

And that is what happened on December 22. The day before, she had told her friends about this man she knew who gave her chewing gum. She showed them a piece of gum in its pretty foreign wrapper. If anyone wanted some, she would ask the man to give her gum for them too. Her friends wanted it: you'd have to be crazy to turn down such pretty chewing gum! *Okay*, Lena had said, *the man will invite me to his house, and I'll ask him to give me gum for everyone.*

The man, who was so generous with the gum, had begun surfacing in Lena's conversation some months before, but without any details. She would not say who he was, where he came from, or where he lived.

On December 22, Natasha Boroshka found her friend Lena Zakotnova at her favorite after-school activity—skating on the icy road. They went home together. On the way they stopped at Natasha's because Lenochka had to "tinkle." After she was done, she announced she was going to see the man with the gum. Natasha stayed home. Along the way Lenochka met another girlfriend. They walked along together for awhile, and then said goodbye until tomorrow.

Until forever, as it turned out.

It was about six o'clock and already dark. A young boy in the same grade as Lena, who had been sent by his father to the pharmacy, saw Lena Zakotnova from behind. She was walking in the direction of the streetcar stop. Alone.

She was seen alive for the last time around six o'clock at the streetcar stop "Trampark," not far from Mezhevoy Lane, on Soviet Street. A middle-aged man in a dark coat and beaver lamb hat, carrying a bag with bottles, was muttering something to the nine-year-old girl in the red coat. The girl's face betrayed confusion. It seemed she was hesitating, unsure whether or not to agree with whatever he was asking. The man, his voice still lowered, continued insisting. Finally, the girl must have made up her mind, for she nodded, and together they set out with the man leading the way.

He opened the gate and, slipping on the snow-encrusted steps, was first to reach the shed. Unlocking the slightly warped door, which opened with a screech, he let the girl in. Only after he had quickly locked and bolted the door behind did he fumble in the darkness for the light switch. A dim bulb hanging from a cord under a filthy, cracking ceiling illuminated the room.

What transpired afterward is known only from the man's own words, recorded in 1990. They corroborate what was found on the girl's body during the investigation. We can only attempt to recreate the scene as he remembered it. Naturally, inaccuracies can creep in—after all, twelve years had passed and it is possible to forget some things.

But he has a good memory. To recognize fifty people by their faces and not make a mistake!

Fifty dead people.

He was more than happy to give a lengthy confession in the investigator's office. These are Chikatilo's words, taken from the case transcripts:

"We entered my bungalow. I turned on the light, as soon as I had locked the door, and immediately pounced on her, crushing her under me. I knocked her to the floor. The girl was frightened and began screaming. I put my hands over her mouth and began to rip off her clothes from below, exposing her body. I unbuttoned her coat. She tore herself away, but there was nothing she could do against me. I lay on top of her, pressing my whole weight down on her body. After I had pulled my pants down, I began to rub my sexual organ against her perineum, but it did not result in an erection of my sexual member, and I was unable to insert it into her vagina. But the desire to satisfy myself eclipsed all reason, and I wanted to achieve this by any means possible. Her screams excited me even more. Laying on top of her and rocking back and forth, as if in imitation of the sexual act, I reached for my knife and began to strike her with it . . . I had an ejaculation . . . as in a natural climax, and I began putting my sperm into her vagina with my hands. With my hands I crawled inside her sexual organs, I felt like ripping and touching everything. She gasped, I strangled her, and this brought a kind of relief. When I realized that I had killed her, I got up, dressed, and decided to get rid of the corpse."

Anyone reading these confessions one after another might suddenly realize—along about the twentieth or thirtieth incident—that he or she has lost the sensation of a never-ending nightmare. The fellow just keeps talking and talking. One case, another, a third. It all seems to fit, and he doesn't appear to be lying.

It is possible that something has been toned down or edited in the transcripts. Still, there is not a single unprintable word or expression. Instead, his speech is riddled with euphemisms and terminology more suitable for medical textbooks than for confessions of sexual crimes and mutilation.

The confessions have not been embellished or censored. The murderer never swore himself, and couldn't tolerate other men who peppered their speech with curses in his presence. Only once, in all his testimony, did he use an indecent word, but for the sake of propriety he wrote it in Roman letters. As a youth, he'd blushed when people used vulgarities in his presence.

Part of this, no doubt, can be attributed to his proper education. He had graduated from Rostov State University with a degree in philology.

* * *

He dressed in a hurry, looked at himself in the mirror to make sure everything was all right and that all traces of blood had been removed. Then he adjusted the clothing on the dead girl. Carefully he wiped the floor of any spots of blood. He lifted the light body and headed toward the door.

He looked around once again to make sure there was nothing he had forgotten. He had—her schoolbag on the floor. He grabbed it, and once again surveyed the room. It appeared everything was in order. He opened the door and stepped out into the darkness— there are no street lights on such lanes as this. Carefully locking the door behind him, he slowly descended the slippery steps leading to the road.

Despite his caution, he committed two mis- takes—the mistakes of a novice. He would never again make such errors. First, he forgot to turn off the light inside. It is difficult to believe that a person who always turns lights off when going out to save money on his electric bill would let such a simple thing slip his mind completely.

This accidental lapse almost cost him his freedom, let alone his life.

It is pitch dark at night on Mezhevoy Lane, but he knew the road well. The place where he decided to go was not far away. The girl did not weigh much, so it was no problem to carry her the distance. However, he placed the corpse on the ground near the house across from his shed to get a better grip on it.

That was his second act of negligence, and, again, it could have tripped him up. . .

About two minutes later he arrived at the bank of the Grushevka River. Slowly he made his way down to the water's edge and placed the body in the water. He tried to avoid getting his shoes wet. He shoved the body from the bank into the current, and tossed the schoolbag in after. The rest, he figured, the current would take care of.

Only by a stretch of the imagination can the Grushevka be called a proper river. At Mezhevoy Lane it is no more than a few feet wide—a brook, at best, but the current is strong. In the winter, due to the melting snow that feeds it, the Grushevka becomes a little wider, though not by much.

The location where he had placed the body in the water is well suited for concealing a body. Puny lopsided fences, concealing garden plots behind, come up to the river. Right on the shore is an abandoned dump, next to the skeleton of a dacha outhouse. Sickly weeping willows grow along the slope. The river bed is incredibly polluted with the carcasses of overturned automobiles, their bald tires protruding out of the water. Amid all this junk flows the river Grushevka. This is where the body was deposited and ultimately found.

★ ★ ★

On the 24th of December, 1978, a resident of Shakhty by the name of Gurenkova was on her way home from work with her colleagues on a streetcar travelling down Soviet Street. Passing over the Grushevsky Bridge, they spotted a small crowd near the river. Policemen's caps could be made out among the assembled figures. In provincial cities, events that are worthy of a crowd's attention, let alone the police, do not occur all that often. The group of co-workers decided to get off at the next stop and see what was going on.

The drowned body of a girl lay on the shore. She had been recently fished out from under the bridge—that same bridge over which the streetcar had just passed. Her schoolbag was there, too. The current had washed it out onto a dry spot downstream. Gurenkova looked at the drowned victim's face and let out a cry: this is the little girl in the red hooded coat she had seen two evenings before. A man with a bag had been standing next to her, and wine bottles had been sticking out of his bag. Gurenkova was certain. Where was it she had seen them? It was at the streetcar stop, at about this time—around six in the evening. No, she couldn't be mistaken. This was the same girl.

Gurenkova related everything to her husband, who was a member of a volunteer patrol group. He immediately reported to the police.

Lena's family, worried and in despair, had been searching two days for her. They identified her instantly. The police tried to keep the facts about the marks of violence on her body from the public.

When a corpse turns up bearing the traces of a violent death—and there were many on the young girl's body—a system immediately goes into effect. The police conduct an inquiry, the prosecutor opens a criminal case, and into its very first folder go the protocols concerning the discovery of the corpse, the conclusion of experts, and the depositions of eyewitnesses.

What Gurenkova had to say about the evening rendezvous at the streetcar stop was also introduced into the case. She turned out to be an observant eyewitness who pointed out the distinctive features of the man with the bag. Sketch artist Vladimir Petrovich Belmasov was called in. A landscape and portraiture artist, who could draw a pretty good picture, he had helped the police solve more than one case in the past. Going by the eyewitness's detailed description, he sketched a portrait of the man. Gurenkova said it looked very much like him.

The man's portrait was photographed, copied and handed out to police around the area with instructions to find and arrest him. For two or three weeks

the police patrolled the city streets in search of a man
with an elongated face and a large nose. They questioned schoolchildren, streetcar conductors, and all
other residents who on the day of the murder might
happened to have seen the suspect. After all,
Gurenkova had spotted him and remembered. Surely
someone else must have come across him—the city
is not all that big.

Accompanied by policemen, Gurenkova also
spent a good deal of time during those days searching
the city, especially those places, like beer stands,
where men usually gather. Maybe she would just hit
upon the real thing there.

Right before New Year's, a senior lieutenant
stopped by the office of I.P. Andreev, director of a
local trade school, and showed him a picture. He
explained that this person was being sought in connection with a young girl's murder.

Without a moment's hesitation, Andreev recognized the face. How could he not recognize a member
of his own teaching staff? He gave the lieutenant the
man's name and address. The lieutenant asked
Andreev not to say a word about this to anyone for
the time being, and hurried off to the police department to report to his superiors. This was not just a
clue, but the suspect himself.

Meanwhile, other policemen were fanning out in
the vicinity near the Grushevka. Not a single house
along Mezhevoy Lane was left unsearched.

The thorough combing also yielded something.
On the very first day some lads from the neighboring

police department found traces of blood near the fence of house number 25. They carefully gathered them. In legal terms, they removed evidence. The chief commissioner of the Shakhty Department of Internal Affairs, V.V. Faimanov, instantly prized the find and drew up a report on the spot.

In house number 24, next door to the shed, lived L.A. Sibiryakova. She had moved there just one month before and still did not know all her neighbors by name. All she knew about her closest neighbor, a tall middle-aged man, was that he worked somewhere as a teacher and lived alone. He was probably a bachelor or divorced. She had heard of Lenochka Zakotnova's disappearance on the radio and was terribly grieved by it, for Lena had been friends with her daughter.

In Shakhty, as in many other Russian cities, there is usually a cinema called "Aurora," named not in honor of the goddess of the dawn but in memory of the legendary battleship which in December 1917, according to the official version, ushered in the era of socialism. This "Aurora" will figure into more than one tragic event. Sibiryakova had gone to an early evening movie on the day of Lena's disappearance. Afterward, at around seven, she had returned home with a friend and noticed that a light was shining through the curtained windows of the shed. *That's good*, she had said to her friend. *Lately the teacher has been home in the evenings and the windows are lit up. Otherwise it's so dark out there you can break both legs if you're not careful.*

After Lena's body had been found in the river, Sibiryakova, like all her neighbors, had been summoned to the nearest police station for questioning. There she bumped right into the teacher. "Pleased to meet you," she said, adding that she was glad too see the lights in the windows. "Now I can at least see the road."

His reply, not very friendly or neighborly, was along the lines of "*I'm afraid you're mistaken, I didn't buy this bungalow for myself but for my elderly father and I only pop in on occasions, just to make sure everything is all right. But I haven't been there in a long time.*"

"How is that?" asked a surprised Sibiryakova. "Just the other day I was on my way home from the movies, and your windows were lit up."

The teacher said nothing, shuffled his feet, and drooped a little around the shoulders. Sibiryakova noticed he began to blink. The police also took note of this: their eyes are well-trained.

The teacher was beginning to look more and more suspicious. He had already been interrogated five times, once in the presence of his wife. The teacher was married and lived with his family, not in some wretched hovel, but in a different place entirely. His wife never had a clue about the other little dwelling that her husband had acquired without her knowledge or approval. This, naturally, caused a minor family scene right there in the station.

The teacher kept getting entangled in his answers. With each new interrogation his replies became less convincing. He contradicted himself. And then, suddenly, the man was left alone.

Later, during the inquest, he would have this to say about it: "They called me down to the police station for questioning. I denied any role in this crime, and they believed me." Whether or not the police believed him, the teacher was no longer called in for questioning.

As for Gurenkova, the sharp-eyed woman who had recognized the teacher—the suspect was not even shown to her. When her husband asked a friend on the police force why, he was told that a mistake had been made in the sketch of the suspect. Besides, the murderer had already been caught and booked.

Director Andreev, who had instantly seen the portrait as a depiction of the teacher from his trade school, was also told not to worry. The real killer was sitting behind bars and had confessed to everything.

CHAPTER 4

The Case of Aleksandr Kravchenko

ACCUSATION (1979-1982)

AMONG THE several dozen inhabitants of Mezhevoy Lane, where the body of Lenochka Zakotnova was found, there lived a person by the name of Aleksandr Kravchenko. There was nothing remarkable about him, although certain activities of his in the past had made him known to the police. Lately, however, he had been keeping a low profile.

Immediately following the murder, but without a perpetrator to show for it, the investigators and detectives began to work up several versions of the crime and approach it from different angles—standard procedure in such events. One group questioned everyone who had seen the girl in the final days and hours of her life. Another reproduced copies of the artist's sketch of the man with the longish nose; still a third conducted a house-to-house search in the vicinity of the Grushevka River.

But the very first order of the day was to have a check of the police files to see if they might turn up any suspicious types, or any previously convicted or arrested individuals who might be worth taking a look at. If such a person were found, his testimony would have to be recorded and his alibi checked out. Again, routine procedure.

With unbelievably good luck, the files turned up twenty-five-year-old Aleksandr Kravchenko. Where did he live? On Mezhevoy Lane, the same dark and rutted street. In which house? One near the river, between the fence and the edge of the water—beyond that is only an abandoned outhouse. Not only that, but he also had a prior conviction—for rape and murder.

If he had not been a minor at the time the offense was committed, he most certainly would have faced capital punishment. Or, as it is called nowadays in Russia, *the exceptional measure*. There is, in fact, nothing exceptional about it at all. Even in good times—by Russian standards—hundreds of executions by a bullet to the head are carried out in the course of a single year. According to information provided by the Russian Ministry of Internal Affairs, 144 death penalties were handed down in 1991, of which 79 were fulfilled. The others were replaced with lengthy sentences. On the other hand, it is a far cry from the 1930s when hundreds of thousands faced "exceptional measures," and still more were condemned to death without trial.

Thus Aleksandr Kravchenko, accused of clauses 102 and 116 of the Criminal Code of Russia, was facing capital punishment, but since he was younger than eighteen at the time, the exceptional measure stipulated by law was commuted to the maximum sentence under the Code—fifteen years. The only fate worse than fifteen years was the exceptional measure—death by shooting.

Kravchenko did not serve out his sentence. The country needed cheap labor. For good behavior, he was first paroled and then sent to work on construction projects. But if he tried to escape, or violate any of the terms set down for him by the police in exchange for his freedom, it would be back to the prison camp for him.

He behaved himself on the job, committed no infractions, and fulfilled his norm at work. As a result, Kravchenko was let go ahead of time because of his conscientious performance, and for confessing to the crime he had been accused of. He set off for Shakhty and took up residence with his woman.

Coincidentally, they settled on Mezhevoy Lane. And not just anywhere—they settled in the very first house adjacent to a vacant lot, right on the shore of the Grushevka. It was as if the police had received an unexpected gift. They arrested Kravchenko immediately.

Yet, his neighbors spoke well of him: he'd seen the error of his ways, he reported to work and hardly ever drank. Whether he was married or not, no one knew—no one went around checking his documents—but he'd been living with the same woman, and they were a family as families go. They did not quarrel and not long ago she had given birth to a child. He related to children well, and overall seemed to be a good sort.

All such statements, however, were only general observations, not proof of innocence. After all, Kravchenko had already committed one murder in the past. Therefore, he might be capable of doing it a second time. There was just one catch—this time around there was not a shred of evidence against Kravchenko, except for the circumstantial fact that he lived right next door to the scene of the crime.

And if there was no evidence, it would have to be found. Investigators know that if an effort is made, something can always be found. There was nothing left to do but try harder. The city was in an uproar and the municipal leaders were beside themselves.

But then an obstacle, at first glance seemingly insurmountable, unexpectedly cropped up—an alibi. Aleksandr Kravchenko had an ironclad, one-hundred-percent alibi. At six o'clock in the evening on the day of Lenochka Zakotnova's death, when, according to Gurenkova's testimony, the girl was still alive, Kravchenko had been on his way home from work and sober as a judge. Two witnesses could vouch for that: his wife and her girlfriend. Both women gave depositions independent of one another, and there was no way they could have colluded between themselves, or with Kravchenko. In such a case, the police

The House of Justice in Rostov-on-Don.

Left: Amurkhan Yandiev, investigator of homicide crimes for the Rostov Regional Office of the Public Prosecutor. He entered the "shelter-belt" case in 1985.

Below: Lieutenant-colonel Viktor Burakov (sitting), head of the Homicide Department of the Rostov Militia Board. He started his search of Chikatilo back in 1982.

Left: Judge Leonid Akubzhanov.

Right: Public prosecutor Anatoly Zadorozhny.

Above: Defense lawyer
Marat Khabibulin.

Right: Psychiatrist
Aleksandr Bukhanovsky.

Militia sergeant Igor Rybakov testifying before the court. It was Rybakov who, on November 6, 1990, checked Chikatilo's papers, and then filed a "suspicious person" report on him.

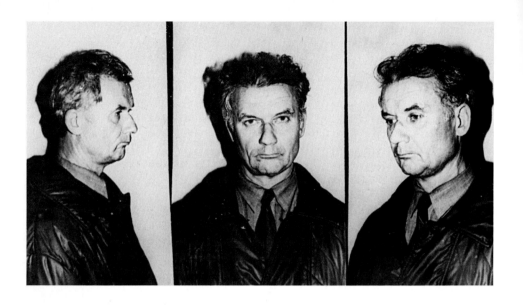

Mug shots of Chikatilo
taken the day he was arrested.

Police drawing used to search for the serial killer.

After Chikatilo was arrested on November 20, 1990, investigators found 23 knives in his flat in Novocherkassk. These were Chikatilo's killing tools.

would have no alternative but to make an apology for false arrest and let the person go immediately.

For the Soviet police, however, there was no such thing as a foolproof alibi.

On a trumped-up charge—one of the neighbors was missing some clothes that had been drying on a line—Kravchenko's wife was brought in to headquarters for a shake-down. It was hinted that if she continued to stick by her husband's alibi, she'd wind up in prison. And not just for theft, but for being an accomplice to murder. There was something fishy, she was told, about the way she was covering up for the murderer. And furthermore, it made no difference whether her husband had an alibi or not—he killed the girl. It could not have been anyone else. After all, it would not be the first time for him. If the woman was going to play stubborn with the police, it would just make things worse for him. She could save his neck by making a voluntary confession and giving him up. He would do his time and return to her, but if she persisted in lying, she was warned, he'd get what was coming to him. Her child would grow up without a father. *Think about your child*, she was told, *if you don't want to think about your husband*.

Kravchenko's wife was in a bind. There was no one to provide her legal counsel. At the time of the arrest, when the investigation proper had not yet begun, it was absurd to even bring up the idea of a lawyer. No one had read her any version of Miranda rights. She knew nothing of the law.

When the interrogation was completed, Kravchenko's wife was not allowed to go home to her child. She was locked up in a cell. By comparison, her shack on Mezhevoy Lane was a palace.

Inevitably, she gave in. No, her husband had not come home at six, but at seven-thirty, and not sober as a judge but pretty well intoxicated.

She was released and sent home.

Now it was her friend's turn. There was no way to pin the laundry theft on her, so what could the police bring her in for? For perjury. Here the logic was even simpler: since Kravchenko's wife had refused to substantiate her husband's alibi, then the friend must not be telling the truth. In other words, she was trying to mislead the authorities while consciously covering up for the murderer at the same time. This was a crime that carried a jail sentence.

They held the woman for seventy-two hours, but she refused to change her story. By law, seventy-two hours was the maximum she could be detained without being formally accused of something. After that, she would have to be let go.

The fourth twenty-four period began, and still the police would not let her go. Out of helplessness and horror, the woman broke down, recanting all her previous testimony. *I don't know anything*, she said, *I didn't see anything. Thank you*, said the police, *just sign here and here, please*. She was set free.

The alibi no longer existed. Now investigators could go after Aleksandr Kravchenko. Right away, he was informed that things would go much better for him if he would just confess to everything. He was taken aback—confess to what? Not to murder—he had never even seen the girl. Showing no outward signs of worry, Kravchenko stuck to his alibi. He had witnesses who had seen him leave work and who had seen him arrive home.

He was not aware that he no longer had any such alibi.

The investigator pressured him, but Kravchenko persisted in his alibi.

The first blow was delivered by his wife who, in a face-to-face meeting with him, showed him everything she had been forced to sign. The second blow he received inside a jail cell and not just one, but dozens of them, well aimed at his head, ribs, kidneys, groin, wherever. The administrator of the beatings was a hulking lug who had been specially planted in Kravchenko's cell for just this purpose.

To be a "decoy" in prison was not a profession, but a specialization. Decoys played the role of agent provocateur, coaxing from suspects secrets large and small, in exchange for various favors. There were plenty of stoolies and eavesdroppers to go around on the outside. Aleksandr Kravchenko's cellmate was of a different breed—his job was not to extort information, but to beat it out of the victim. He had received his orders and carried them out.

The investigators' "volunteer" made life for the unfortunate prisoner pure hell. Each day, he was beaten in his cell and humiliated. The thug threatened to "rooster" him, which in prison slang meant to rape him. Just to get out of there, a person would confess to anything, including parricide.

Aleksandr Kravchenko did not hold out for long. He confessed to the murder.

His confession alone, however, was insufficient for the court. Something objective was needed. If there was no evidence, it meant that it was poorly sought. The investigators would put a little effort into it, and surely they would come up with something.

They did. Nettles from bushes, which grow along the banks of the Grushevka, were discovered on Kravchenko's pants. In retrospect, it is hard to believe that such an inconsequential clue could cost Aleksandr Kravchenko his life.

It should have been obvious that a person who lives just a few feet away from some prickly bushes can brush up against them, without intending to commit murder. Moreover, Amurkhan Yandiev, detective in the Rostov prosecutor's office for violent crimes, did not doubt for a moment that this flimsy evidence had been fabricated by the investigation. Really, how long would it have taken to dispatch a sergeant to the Grushevka, have him pluck some nettles and attach them to the suspect's confiscated pants?

But there was something else a bit more serious. The public prosecutor for the case presented to the court expert analysis that established Kravchenko's sweater as having traces of the same blood type as the victim, as well as microscopic particles of her clothing.

Today, one wonders where they came from, and whether they existed at all? Now that Aleksandr Kravchenko has been completely absolved of any wrongdoing in this matter, such questions are strictly academic in nature. His life cannot be returned. Whether he was good or bad is open to discussion, but it is probable there were no traces of Lena Zakotnova's blood, or particles of her clothing, on his person.

Kravchenko tried to resist: "I signed confessions of guilt only because I had heard threats directed against me by several employees of the criminal investigation department and the prison. I learned about certain details of the crime from the minutes of expert analysis—therefore there are certain details, which I learned from the investigators, in my statements made under duress." It was all to no avail. He had already made his confession; nothing else was needed.

During the trial that followed, it was also obvious that the wrongfully accused had been coerced. He even became entangled in his answers, like a student who has not learned his lessons. He erred in telling the victim's age, he could not remember what she was wearing, and he could not say where he had concealed the knife. He even altered his testimony concerning the murder site several times.

The verdict was handed down—Aleksandr Kravchenko was sentenced to death.

For a long time, his fate swung back and forth on the scales of Russian justice. The case migrated from Rostov to Moscow and back again. On several occasions, it was resubmitted to further inquiry. Nothing new was brought to light, and not one single clue was added.

In December 1980, the bar of the Supreme Court of Russia commuted Aleksandr Kravchenko's death penalty to a term of fifteen years. But in August 1981 the highest judicial body in Russia, the Presidium of the Supreme Court, again ruled that the case be opened to further investigation. In spring of 1992 it was heard for one more time. Although this second inquest did not provide any new evidence of guilt against Kravchenko, the bar of the Rostov Court once again—finally and irrevocably—pronounced the death penalty.

Many years later, the judge who had rendered the verdict would say, "At the time I had no doubts whatsoever concerning Kravchenko's guilt."

The Supreme Court let the verdict stand.

The Presidium of the Supreme Court denied any requests for clemency.

On March 23, 1983, twenty-nine-year-old Aleksandr Kravchenko was executed by a firing squad.

In 1991 the Supreme Court of the Russian Federation, upon the fourth hearing of the case, rescinded the sentence that had been carried out eight years earlier.

CHAPTER 5

The Case of Aleksandr Kravchenko

ACQUITTAL (1991)

IN OTHER PLACES, in other times, the story of the execution of an innocent person would rock society and provide grist for discussion and attacks in the press. It would bring reflection on the theme of iniquity in the courts, and condemnation of the failings of the third branch of government.

In this case nothing of the sort occurred. Two or three articles passed swiftly by, something was broadcast over the radio, and official apologies were offered to Kravchenko's mother. Nothing more.

Let us now return to the main character—the one with the long nose and face, the owner of the shed at 26 Mezhevoy Lane—Andrei Chikatilo.

When the teacher was brought in for questioning and the whole bloody chain of events was rolled out before him, he began to talk. At his own initiative, he confessed to one crime after another, even reporting on some murders that the investigators had no

71

inkling of, and about still others for which the perpe-
trators had been sought for many years but which
had never been linked to him.

Two months after his arrest, in the beginning of
1991, he recalled that in the winter of 1978 he had
killed a girl in Shakhty.

"The murder of this little girl was my first crime.
Without any prompting, I candidly related the circumstances of her death. At the time of arrest in connection with the present case, the investigative
bodies could not have known that this murder had
been committed by me. After I had made the decision
to speak candidly about all the crimes I had committed, I decided to tell all from the very beginning—
that is, from this first murder, for it was precisely
after this crime that I began to murder my other victims. However, during the first interrogation sessions, I could not speak truthfully about the murder
site of Zakotnova, because at that time my family
was living in Shakhty, and if I had said that I had
killed her in the outbuilding, the residents of this
city could have easily found and destroyed my
family.

"Later I found out that the members of my family
had changed their last name and left Shakhty, and
after this, I began to give more accurate testimony
concerning the site of the murder of this young girl. I
even showed them the site."

He did not confuse any details. He had an excellent memory. He testified at first that he had committed the murder right on the shore of the

Grushevka—he didn't have the patience, he said, to get her back to his house. He was concerned for his relatives, fearing mob justice. Later, he told about the murder in all its details. It appeared to be the truth. Everything checked out.

The suspect voluntarily confessed to the murder of Lena Zakotnova. But now the investigation was being led by others. There had been a changing of the guard, and the case entered a new phase.

The new investigator in charge, Amurkhan Yandiev, did not believe the confession. He wanted proof. He set out for Shakhty in search of it.

After so many years, it could not have been an easy task to find the eyewitnesses and witnesses whose testimony had been filed with the case. But with the Russian system of keeping the population's mobility restricted through any number of official passes, it should not have been particularly difficult, either.

Much more difficult, as it turned out, was for Yandiev to get his hands on Kravchenko's case. He was given the runaround and refused for various reasons. He was not the only one. His colleague from Moscow, Issa Kostoyev, an investigator in the violent crimes division of the Rostov prosecutor's office—who for years had headed the investigative team in search of the serial killer and who had publicly sworn to restore Kravchenko's innocence—was able to obtain Kravchenko's case from the archives only after expending great effort and cutting through layers of red tape.

The outrageous miscarriages of justice were discovered almost as soon as the case had been turned
over to the new investigators. When, at the end of the
1970s, evidence had been stubbornly procured that
would damn Aleksandr Kravchenko as the murderer,
anything else that could have provided even the
slightest hint of there being an accomplice to the
crime was removed from the investigative materials
and buried in other files. Not all materials are
admitted into court. Since it is the prosecutor who
brings the case to court, whatever comes up in the
course of the investigation and inquiry, or whatever
incidental and circumstantial evidence is revealed,
are internal matters not for public record. The court
is not obliged to know everything.

But had the court known more than it did, the
version put forth by the investigation might not have
held up. The investigators were the ones who had
decided what the court should know and what
should be kept secret.

At the end of the 1970s, no one in either the
Rostov Court or the Supreme Court had any inkling
about the man with the wine bottles in his bag, about
the unextinguished light in the cottage, or about the
director of the trade school who had instantly recognized his teacher from the police sketch. Nor did
anyone know about the traces of blood found near
house No. 25, even though Faimanov's report was
available. In fact, it was as if there were no blood
traces at all!

The only problem was that the report did not lay
in the investigative files, but with the operative

materials. And for unknown reasons, it never even occurred to anyone at the time to line up the teacher and Kravchenko in front of Gurenkova for identification. No one thought to look around inside the house, where lights had been burning in the windows that evening, or perhaps search the floor for traces of blood.

Amurkhan Yandiev was forty-four when he took on the case, forty-eight when it went to trial. He is a short and wiry Ingush, an ethnic minority from the Caucasus region, with the characteristic mashed ears of a freestyle wrestler. In his day he had enjoyed some successes on the wrestling mat. Indeed, many of the boys from that part of the country dream of someday becoming championship wrestlers. Stubborn as a mule, Yandiev prefers legwork to a desk job. He likes to visit a place and engage the locals in informal conversation. He wears out a lot of shoe leather in a day—he still does not have an official car, though he is always being promised that he will be sold a Zhiguli for personal use and that his gas expenses will be covered.

Untwisting the case of the teacher and simultaneously reconstructing Kravchenko's, he spent weeks walking around Shakhty from street to street, from house to house, during which time he was able to find out quite a bit.

The obdurate Russian people are not overly keen on giving testimony or cooperating with the police, nor do they have any great desire to get involved in official investigations. Anyone who has been "ironed out" by the Soviet punitive machine does not willingly get mixed up with it unless it is a matter of dire emergency.

The old women of Shakhty, the *babushki*, did not want to talk to the man from the prosecutor's office. But Amurkhan was in no hurry. He would park himself on a bench in front of an apartment building and strike up idle conversation about life in general, about the insane prices nowadays, about the small pensions and about the children and grandchildren who no longer showed their elders any respect, although you couldn't blame them under the circumstances—they were not the ones responsible for this life.

Thus, in the course of conversations and gossip, Yandiev came to know about the woman from Mezhevoy Lane who, long before Lena's murder had seen a girl, about age ten, dashing from the teacher's outbuilding in the direction of Soviet Street. Not Lena—a different one. The woman proved to have a good memory and related everything as if it had all happened yesterday: "Her eyes were bulging out of her head in fear, she was barefoot, it was summer, and running toward a streetcar, and right behind her was this guy, holding on to his pants to keep them from falling."

The woman sensed something was wrong and yelled to the girl to run into her house, but the girl didn't hear her because at that moment a streetcar passed by. The girl leaped into the car, the doors closed behind her, and the streetcar continued on.

Yandiev tried to find this girl, who by now was grown up and perhaps even married. He searched the whole city for her but he didn't find her. No one remembered anything. Or did no one want to remember? "What was it that happened here?" Yandiev asked himself. "You can understand why. Any normal person would try to suppress such memories and not have to relive them again. I keep thinking, thank God the streetcar arrived in time."

In the summer and fall of 1978, plenty of bloody traces were to be found in the small city of Shakhty. "During that period I was irresistibly drawn to children," Chikatilo would later testify. "I had a desire to see their naked bodies, their sexual organs. I wanted to have sexual intercourse with them, but already by then my potency was diminished. What else had an effect, apparently, was the fact that when I moved to Shakhty and found employment at State Professional Trade School No. 33, my family stayed behind in Novoshakhtinsk and for awhile I was like a vagrant, a wanderer.

"During that period, I was often in the center of town where there were always many children. I visited one school after another. I would walk right in and always find out where the bathroom is. Since I was more attracted to girls, I tried to stand closer to the girls' room and, when nobody was looking, I would go in and spy on the children. There were times when I was caught at such activities. When that happened, I would immediately leave without making a sound.

"In order to get the children to come up to me, I would sometimes treat them to gum, just so they would spend some time alone with me. I don't remember to whom specifically I gave gum, but on this basis I got to know the children."

Yandiev managed rather quickly to find witnesses who had driven the wanderer from the school toilets on more than one occasion. Even then, they knew that the kindly "gent," about forty years old or so, was irresistibly drawn to children and who, in exchange for their friendship, would offer them foreign gum—hard currency to children in Russia.

G.G. Ishchenko, who worked at the time as a vice principal at School No. 10, unhesitatingly recognized the teacher from the many photographs Yandiev had shown her from the police files. What had prevented anyone from plastering the city that winter with the sketch of his face? Especially in view of the fact that Andreyev, director of the trade school, had also instantly recognized his teacher.

Naturally, Yandiev paid a visit to Andreyev. He had suffered a stroke and was no longer employed as director. Yandiev learned from him a most curious detail: after being visited only one time by someone from the police department, no one ever again showed any interest in either him or the teacher. Not once. Careless work can be found in any walk of life, but considering the crime it is difficult to believe the existence of such incredible unprofessionalism. In contrast, Yandiev's investigative team conscientiously performed all duties demanded of its profession and executed all routine procedures.

At their insistence, a physical and technical examination was conducted. It confirmed that the stab wounds found on Lena's body could have been made, with a high degree of certainty, by one of the twenty-three knives that turned up during a search of the teacher's last apartment. Precisely, knife designated No. 22.

Moreover, Yandiev accompanied the teacher to the cottage that was once his and had long since been sold for next to nothing. Before a video camera, using a mannequin he confidently demonstrated how he had acted, how he had held the victim and how he had struck with the knife. He left nothing out and did not get mixed up in his testimony, unlike Aleksandr Kravchenko. He even willingly elucidated certain details which up until then had confounded the investigation.

When Lena's body had been pulled from the Grushevka, her eyes were tightly bound by her own scarf. Blindfolds are usually applied to a victim's eyes to keep the victim from seeing the road and recognizing it later. But the girl had voluntarily gone to the man's dwelling, so there would be no reason to cover her eyes along the way. This meant he had bound her eyes afterward. Perhaps, after the murder had been done, he remembered an old superstition, according to which a dead person's retina is marked by the last thing he sees before dying—in this case, the terrible face of murder?

"At the time of committing the crime I bound Zakotnova's eyes with a scarf, since I was terrified of seeing her look."

In general, he could not look people in the eye for long. He averted his gaze at staff meetings, when he was handed assignments or was lectured for shortcomings in his work. He also could not bear the stares of students in school or his subordinates in the supply division where he worked after changing professions.

Thus, he could not look his victims in the eye. Not this one, his first, nor the many others to follow. So he blinded them.

He bound the first victim's eyes. With his subsequent victims he left a strange pattern of stab wounds around their eyes. These later came to be identified as part of the Rostov killer's "signature." Experts compared them with the knives from the teacher's extensive collection and made the following conclusion: "The possibility cannot be excluded that the wounds were made by the same instrument. It is highly likely that it was knife No. 22."

* * *

It is a wonderful thing when justice triumphs. Even if it comes twelve years later, even after several dozen innocent deaths. But why did it take so long?

Way back in the beginning of 1979, everything could have fallen into place. The frightened teacher, put on the spot by numerous witnesses, would hardly

have kept his silence for long. True, there were no
direct eyewitnesses, but there was more than enough
circumstantial evidence. He would turn flushed then
pale, stammer and blink his small eyes during the
first interrogation sessions. He would sweat and then
clam up.

There would have been no need to destroy
Aleksandr Kravchenko's alibi by illicit means. The
real murderer did not have any alibi at all. He left
more than his fair share of tracks behind. Any private
detective, bucking for a promotion, could not have
dreamed of such a dilettante criminal.

Any number of suppositions about what happened
to let Chikatilo slip away can now be offered. The
first one is rather serious. Let us assume that at the
time Chikatilo had some powerful sponsors who had
the right to say "Hands off!" Such things did happen
during the Soviet years, but to cover up for a murderer even in the worst of times was not always a
risk worth taking. If the person was not of any particular value, it was easier just to hand him over and be
done with it.

The transcripts of the case show that, a year
before he committed his first murder, Chikatilo had
become a volunteer helper, a freelance employee—
read: informer—for the ministry of internal affairs.
That is, the police. In addition, during his years in
the army he had served in Berlin, in special communication troops, on the KGB's Berlin to Moscow wire.

Specialists such as these, even after their dis-
charge, do not walk away from the KGB just like

that. They know too much. For a long time afterward, they are kept on a short leash. Rumor has it that in the 1980s, Chikatilo, who was then working as a supply clerk, made use of travel warrants issued for his numerous trips around the country. Such warrants are only handed out to the chosen few who travel on special assignment and truly cannot waste valuable business time standing on long lines for tickets. And travel warrants are issued to the special services.

This is only speculation on the part of the authors. We have no concrete evidence that he worked for the KGB. But, on the other hand, why would he not have served them in some capacity? After all, he was a party member, a graduate from the higher institutions of Marxism-Leninism, robust and energetic. And if it were discovered he had a little fault—a certain unhealthy attraction for minors, to put it delicately—so what? Nobody was perfect. It was even better when they came with flaws—that made it easier to keep them on a tight leash.

There was still one more consideration. In spite of the difficulties imposed by the Soviet bureaucratic system of moving from one place to another, Chikatilo was able to change cities and apartments very easily, suspiciously easy. To the envy of his neighbors, he was given official apartments—this in a country where people can wait an entire lifetime for housing! His purchase in March 1978 of the shed on Mezhevoy Lane from citizeness Fesenko for a song also appears a bit suspicious against the backdrop of the country's thorny housing problems. He had bought a small dwelling on the cheap, maybe not in the capital but not in some godforsaken little village either, and no one—not his family nor his coworkers—knew anything about it.

People who are extremely well-informed about the case—such as Yandiev, for example—listen to the hypothesis about the teacher's dealings with the dark activities of the KGB with a smile on their lips. Perhaps there really is no connection with "Galina Borisovna," as the Committee for State Security is known among the people. Still, perhaps there is.

There is one more supposition which, from the authors' point of view, is totally groundless, but since it is discussed in certain circles with all seriousness it must be mentioned. A youth newspaper in southern Russia, *Nashi Vremena,* "Our Times," called the defendant in an editorial in July 1992, while the trial was in progress, "Satan" in the literal sense of the word. According to the paper, the maniacal killer belonged to a cult of satanists who cured impotency by devouring the sexual organs of young people. The diagram of wounds on the corpses revealed satanic "signatures." In concluding, the paper said that it wanted to reject all this mystical nonsense and rely solely upon the scientific facts and results of the courts' medical expertise, but the defendant had called himself Satan.

Maybe Chikatilo truly is a creature from hell. And, if so, perhaps from time to time, an unearthly dark force hid him from the police and kept him from justice. After all, he was no stranger to mysticism. There was the time, for example, in Rostov, when he lured a trusting Natalia Golosovskaya into Aviators' Park. She resisted and screamed. Even though people had been passing nearby—the murderer clearly heard their voices and distinguished their words—not a single one of them heard the sounds of a struggle or the cries for help.

He would explain it this way: "At times I felt like I was concealed from other people by a black hood, which only allowed sounds in, and this hood protects me."

Back then, though, it was all much simpler. The police did not need any more clues or witnesses—in Kravchenko they had in hand a completely suitable candidate for the murders, and this Kravchenko was certainly no sweetheart. All they had to do was apply a little pressure, and he had begun to sing. Chikatilo, on the other hand, was a card-carrying party member with diplomas and a steady job. The best thing to do was to let him go and get the case into court.

Meanwhile, in December of 1978, while an innocent man was being executed, the pitiful wretch with the higher education, loitering in school toilets like a peeping Tom, had become a murderer. He had experienced the smell of blood. He believed there was nothing better than blood to satisfy his lust, that blood aroused him, and that he derived pleasure from it.

But the main thing he understood then was that an educated person, with subtly organized and unusual desires, could and should achieve satisfaction in accordance with his nature and without any nasty consequences. There was no need to rush things. He would have to wait for the appropriate moment.

He raped and murdered his next victim two and a half years later.

CHAPTER 6

Terrible Finds, Futile Searches

1981-1984

ROSTOV-ON-DON, like many other Russian cities developed along the banks of large and small rivers, stretches out in a rather broad strip along one riverbank. This, at least, protects it on one side from unexpected attacks. Walls with guard towers can then be erected to defend the other three sides. The ruins of such a fortress are still to be found in Rostov's former outskirts, nowadays its center. From the top floors of apartment houses there, one can see large and small buildings sloping toward the wide river below. On the other side is an idyllic rural landscape of fields, groves, and reservoirs.

The left bank of the Don, or "Levberdon" as it is called by the Rostov residents—in the typically Soviet fashion of making compound words out of several truncated ones—is a place just across the bridge from Rostov for taking walks or sunning on the beach.

On September 4, 1981, the completely naked corpse of a young girl was found in the shelterbelt on Levberdon, near a cafe that sits on a heavily traveled road. The body had been covered with July's newspapers. The criminal investigation department immediately combed the vicinity. Without much difficulty, they discovered a woman's red jacket, dress, and shredded underwear. They also found a six-foot-long stick covered with traces of blood.

This was one of those murders that could be called nothing else but savage: countless abrasions and bruises over the whole body, the right breast without its nipple, and disembowelment which took place, in the experts' opinion, after death had occurred. Pieces of wood, from that same bloody stick, were found in the girl's vagina and rectum. Death, by strangulation, had come a little bit before.

Her identity was established quickly: Larisa Tkachenko, sixteen years old, a vocational school student. On the day she was killed, she and her schoolmates were supposed to have gone to a state collective farm outside town to help bring in the harvest. It was a rare occasion when a student could get out of these mandatory fall activities. The work was not very taxing, but there was nothing especially pleasant about it either.

Larisa returned to her village to get some warm clothing before going back to Rostov. But she never made it to the school, from where the bus would be leaving to take the students to the farm. Her friends, not overly worried about her absence, had left without her. Maybe something happened at home, or maybe she just decided to skip out.

* * *

Almost one year later, June 12, 1982, twelve-year-old Lyuba Biryuk disappeared from the *stannitsa*, a Cossack settlement, of Zaplavskaya. Her mother, leaving for work, had sent the girl to the nearest settlement of Donskoi, as she had done so often before, to buy food and cigarettes. Her stepfather met her at the bus station near the store. Lyuba was wearing a white floral dress and sandals. No one ever saw her again. A search turned up nothing. The girl was classified as missing—until the following summer.

The following summer—July 27, 1983, to be precise—a corpse was found in a shelterbelt stretching along the highway from Novocherkassk to Bagaievka, not too far from the settlement of Donskoi. It had been lying there at least a year and presented a grisly spectacle. The body—or what was left of it—was naked and had been covered with clumps of grass. Experts concluded that these were the remains of a girl who, without question, had died a violent death from numerous stab wounds to the head, neck and chest. Overall, they counted twenty-two wounds delivered, in all probability, by a knife sharpened on one side. Knife marks were also discovered in the eyesockets.

White sandals were found near the body. Lyuba Biryuk's mother recognized them. She was spared the sight of the body—there was nothing to identify.

* * *

On August 14, 1982, H.P. Oleinikova reported her nine-year-old grandson Oleg Pozhidayev missing to the police department of the city of Krasnodar. The boy had come from Leningrad to visit his grandfather. The day before he had gone to the beach and not come back.

The boy's case was assigned No. 4226. No traces of the boy were ever found, and in December 1988 he was proclaimed dead. The case was closed. If they had not found him after six years, what was the point in searching any longer?

* * *

On October 27, 1982, serviceman Ya.V. Shumei came across a completely nude, decomposed corpse partially covered with foliage. It was found not too far from the Kazachii Lagerya platform on the Rostov-Shakhty line, in a shelterbelt along the railroad tracks. With military precision, Shumei informed his superiors immediately.

Experts concluded it was a young woman, aged sixteen to nineteen, who had died of aggravated injury from a multitude of stab wounds to the vessels of the neck, heart and lungs.

It was later revealed that her name was Olga Kuprina and that she was sixteen years old. She was no angel—she smoked and went with boys. On August 10 she had quarreled with her mother and left home in the farmstead of Baklanniki in the Semikarakorsky region of Rostov province. She did not return. For a week, she lived in the neighboring farmstead with her girlfriend Natalia Shalopinina (she too would disappear, two years later, and her corpse would be found under some trees). Olga had gone with her friend to the bus station, intending to go to Rostov and from there take a commuter train to see her aunt in Shakhty. She had bought her ticket, said goodbye to her friend, and disappeared.

* * *

On September 21, 1982, in a shelterbelt near a remote station platform on the Shakhtnaya-Kirpichnaya stretch of rail—the last stretch before reaching Shakhty—the disfigured corpse of nineteen-year-old Irina Karabelnikova was found. Her torn and bloody clothing was discovered alongside her. The girl's father later placed a memorial on this spot. Vandals came along and smashed it, but the father restored it. This marker, covered with flowers, can still be seen from the window of the train that runs from Rostov to Moscow.

* * *

Ten-year-old Olya Stalmachenok did not make it to class in music school. Her corpse was found four months later lying in a field under a high voltage wire pole near Novoshakhtinsk.

* * *

A retarded youngster named Laura Sarkisyan ran away from home and did not return. Her body was found in a wooded area near a platform, marked simply as "1130 km," on the Kirpichnaya-Shaktnaya rail stretch.

* * *

In Rostov's Aviators' Park, which extends along the road linking the bus station to the airport, the nude, partially decomposed corpse of Irina Dunenkova, a thirteen-year-old girl suffering from Down's syndrome, was found with numerous knife wounds.

* * *

The body belonging to a twenty-four-year-old vagrant named Lyudmila Kutsyuba, the mother of two children, was discovered on that same accursed Shakhtnaya-Kirpichnaya stretch of rail.

* * *

Eight-year-old Igor Gudkov was found in Aviators' Park on August 9, 1983.

* * *

There were others—too many others—who died under similar circumstances and suffered the same horrendous fates, but somehow it still did not occur to anyone at the time that the corpses, with their telltale patterns of knife wounds and missing organs, were links in a single chain. The signature was similar and the motives all seemed to be sexual, but there was not a single eyewitness nor any direct evidence. Today it is known that the blood of these young people is on the hands of one person, but who could have known that back in the summer of 1983?

Imagine being in the place of the people who, by accident or as a result of their duties, came across either still fresh, or partially decomposed, or skeletal human remains.

Someone—a soldier, a trackwalker, a schoolboy, a hunter or an elderly woman—who was walking through a grove, a shelterbelt, or an urban park, would suddenly stumble across a dead body. Nude, moreover, and covered in blood, or with the numbing features of decomposition. A terrible corpse, covered in foliage and newspapers.

Horror would be the most common and natural reaction of any normal person. And horror would drive a person to call the police.

If the incident occurs in a city, a member of the criminal investigation bureau, along with various experts, are called. If it is in a village, more likely than not only a single district militia officer shows up, or maybe he'd grab a couple of witnesses to take along. The more experienced police officers step around the corpse, taking photographs, combing the area nearby, gathering samples of soil and grass, searching for fingerprints and other clues. The rookies, seeing such ghastly sights for the first time, usually take a few steps back and vomit. Sooner or later, the corpse is loaded onto a special vehicle and carted off to the morgue.

After that comes the routine work. Reports are written, the identities of the victims are established, and the private detectives walk around the vicinity in search of any witnesses, or rummage through the files of missing persons. Questioning, cross-questioning, and more questioning again. It is a huge break for the police when, after a fresh body has been found, a drunkard turns up in the house next door with blood stains on his jacket and the victim's money in his pocket, and the neighbors all agree that the two had been drinking vodka the night before and one had promised the other he'd kill him if he did not pay back his debt. It was not even proper to call this detective work. Rare is the case indeed when an obvious candidate for murder reveals himself before the detectives—like Aleksandr Kravchenko.

There were no suspects in the region where the corpses had been discovered. Furthermore, it was not clear what had led the victims to a shelterbelt, a park or a field. There was no single plausible motive for all these crimes. Clues and material evidence, which could have led to the criminal, were mostly absent, but not in every case. There were, for example, old newspapers spread out over Larisa Tkachenko's body. But these same newspapers were read by hundreds of thousands, if not millions, of citizens every day.

The victims were not found near their homes or the homes of their friends and relatives, but in strange places. Many among them were unfortunate individuals, or children of broken families: runaways, prematurely grown-up girls with loose morals, or even retarded children. But other victims were intelligent and came from good, tight-knit families. There were some families who did not notice right away that a son or daughter was missing or who, when they did, failed to report it to the police. It even happened that a family would learn of a child's disappearance from the police long after that child had died.

* * *

Lt. Viktor Vasilyevich Burakov heads the section for serious sexual crimes in the Rostov criminal investigation bureau. He started working on these serial murders in 1983, beginning with the case of Lyuba Biryuk. By year's end he had eleven unsolved corpses on his hands.

"My son at the time was eleven years old," Lt. Burakov, a graying, solidly built man of forty-six, said. "A detective's son is in the same danger as anyone else's child. So are his wife and daughter. We couldn't sleep nights. Literally. Once, after ten sleepless nights in a row, I ended up in the hospital for a month with a nervous breakdown. For five or six years now the whole department has not had any time off. That's fifty people. There were times when despair set in, though we continued to work feverishly."

In the first five months of 1992, a total of 8,364 premeditated murders were committed in Russia. For every thousand murders committed in Russia each year, almost four hundred are attributed to Rostov and its nearest cities. When compared proportionally to the general population, this figure is above average. In both absolute and relative terms, it is a lot—and yet understandable.

Rostov has always had a relatively high crime rate. From earliest times, the southern Russian cities of Rostov and Odessa have been haven not just to petty thieves, pickpockets and swindlers of various stripe, but to major crooks, big-time bandits and criminal gangs who managed to avoid the law for many years. There is even a saying that the locals like to point out to visitors that goes, "If Odessa is the mother of crime, then Rostov is the father."

Rostov-on-Don stands by itself among the southern cities, located at the crossroads of major arteries from north to south, from east to west. People and goods flow through it from Moscow to the Caucasus, from the Volga region to the Crimea, from the Urals to the Black Sea, from Ukraine to Central Asia. People and goods flow through it. Here a person can get rich overnight and lose it all in a second. Here guns, drugs and hard currency are accumulated.

Here tribes and peoples mix together. Here is a southern Russian Babylon.

Back in the beginning of the 1980s, the number of murders, judging by statistics, was somewhat lower than today, though not by much. But even against this joyless backdrop, the crimes that were committed in the shelterbelts and on the outskirts of the city looked especially abominable. These were savage, inconceivably cruel crimes that involved wounds by the dozen on the corpses, whose mouths had been filled with dirt, their eyes poked out, nipples cut or bitten off, sexual organs cut out and removed from the crime scenes, or stuffed into disemboweled bellies.

The top brass of the Rostov criminal investigation department finally began to realize that the local detectives, used to petty thefts and fistfights among drunks, were simply not up to handling such refined crimes that were without clues, motives or witnesses. Belatedly, or so it seems in hindsight, they began to look at the series of unsolved murders as having a single criminal signature. Finally, they made a decision to unite into one case the separate murders of Igor Gudkov and Ira Dunenkova in Rostov, Lyuba Biryuk in the settlement of Donskoi near Novocherkassk, Olya Stalmachenok in Novoshakhtinsk, and the two young women unknown at the time (later revealed to be Ira Karabelnikova and Olya Kuprina) in the shelterbelts near the Shakhtnaya and Kazachii Lagerya stations.

In order to assign the case a code name, something characteristic or common to all the incidents had to be established. Here it was the geographical feature that provided the common thread. The case was nicknamed *Lesopolosa*, "Shelterbelt."

If all the murders hung on the conscience of one person, it had to be understood or at least theorized what led him to do it, why he had a need to do it. What aroused him to rape young girls and boys and then kill them so perversely?

There was no need to search for complex answers if simple ones would do. The simplest answer to come immediately to mind was that the person was abnormal. This vampire, this cannibal, this sex maniac, was mentally ill. A mentally sound person would not be capable of such a thing. More convincing theories could not be found, so this one, the first, became the working version.

A new routine began. An unbelievably boring, monotonous job, but one that was absolutely necessary in view of the circumstances. At least that was how it seemed at the time. All persons registered in psychiatric wards were declared suspects. One by one they were checked out—where they had been lately, and with whom. One by one, their diagnoses and the peculiarities of their illnesses, their behavior under stress and inclination to violence and sexual anomalies, and their alibis at the time the crimes were committed, were examined closely. But all this was incidental. The main thing—the most important thing—that interested the detectives was their blood types. It was the only reliable evidence. Everything else was on the level of supposition.

More victims were added to the case. They were studied more carefully and from time to time sperm, in sufficient amounts for analysis, was recovered from the bodies. It was taken from the victims' ripped and tattered clothing, from their skin, from inside their vaginas and rectums. Each time the medical expertise concluded that the sperm belonged to the antigen group AB. That is, it contained both antigens—A and B—characteristic of a person's blood and secretions. This is the so-called fourth blood type, suitable only for transfusions with patients having the same type and no one else. True, these patients enjoy a privileged position for, if an unknown murderer were to turn up in a hospital suffering from a great loss of blood, the doctors could pour any blood available back into him. But he would not be particularly valued as a donor.

Criminologists had always considered it axiomatic that a person's blood, sperm and all other secretions containing albumen—saliva, for example—all belong to the same type. It was supposed to be genetically predetermined. Consequently, the criminal—or criminals, if there were more than one acting in tandem—had to have blood belonging to type AB.

This led to the main test, which was a blood analysis to determine type affiliation. Every suspect, no matter how farfetched, for the rapes and murders, had blood samples taken from him. If a suspect's blood did not show positive for the fourth type, he was immediately let go with apologies. And in the special file, put together for this case, a notation was made: checked in connection with Operation Shelterbelt.

But if the blood type matched, then the check-up continued. Next, the alibis were examined, movements monitored, and psychiatrists consulted until they were convinced the suspect was definitely not a party to murder. It was long, tedious and, worst of all, fruitless work. Hundreds of people had to be checked simultaneously from psychiatric hospitals and detention cells. And if someone was beginning to look like the one, then his blood type did not match or his alibi was impeccable.

In order to keep track of all the suspects who were checked, verified, and released, a data base was set up to record the names of all the suspects checked in connection with Operation Shelterbelt. But it was not a data base set up in a computer—all data were handwritten on index cards. Computerization was something the Rostov investigators could only hope for in their wildest dreams. The card index, which eventually swelled to more than 25,000 cards, still sits in Burakov's office. The ninth card in the index refers to "Chikatilo, Andrei Romanovich" and dates to his first arrest in 1984. A note on the card said that he had been exempted from further suspicion because his blood type did not match the type of the killer the police were after.

Then suddenly—success.

In the beginning of September 1983, a young man was detained by the police in the Rostov streetcar depot where he had no business being. His name was Shaburov. Held in the precinct for twenty-four hours for the sake of propriety, he was about to be let go when suddenly he made a voluntary and startling confession: he and his mate Kalenik had stolen an automobile. And, after a short pause, he made a second confession which stunned the investigators: the two of them had killed children.

Why? No reason. They had killed because they liked it. His confederate was arrested on the spot, and two others immediately thereafter: Turov and Korzhov. They had also killed. All of them together, and each on his own.

All four of them were mentally defective. Not insane to the point where they were incapable of answering for their actions, but not quite normal nonetheless.

Thus, the police now had a quartet of candidates for murder: V. Shaburov, Y. Kalenik, L. Turov and L. Korzhov. All four lived in the Pervomaisky district of Rostov, the same district where Aviators' Park is located. They had all attended the same boarding school for retarded children. Having completed their studies, they had remained at the boarding school. Where were they to go, without parents and relatives, mentally unsound, and no homes of their own?

Their arrest set off a two-year investigation, code-named by investigators in both Moscow and Rostov, without any irony or quotations, *delo durakov*, the case of the fools.

The word "fool" in the richly nuanced Russian language can have many meanings. It can be a term of contempt but it can also have tender connotations. In Russian folklore, Ivanushka the fool plays the role of simpleton and clumsy oaf on the outside, but in fact he is smarter and wilier than everyone else. A mother is perfectly capable of calling her child "my little fool" while stroking its head. In harshest terms, it refers to one who is mentally ill or insane. The popular name for a psychiatric hospital is *durdom*, "fool's house."

Chikatilo, incidentally, also spent some time undergoing observation in the main "fool's house" in the country, the infamous Serbsky Institute, officially named the V.P. Serbsky All-Union Scientific Research Institute of General and Forensic Psychiatry. Many people, from inveterate criminals to dissidents against the Soviet regime, have spent time there. In spite of its unfortunate notoriety, more political than medical, this institute still commands authority in the world's scientific community, and the opinions of its experts are held in esteem.

After only four days since their arrest, Kalenik had already confessed to seven murders. It seemed that he, too, had accomplices. One after another, Tyapkin, Ponamarev and Velichko, all from the same boarding school, were brought in. Rumors spread throughout the city about a band of maniacs. The criminal case swelled with more and more new materials, many of which did not stand up to criticism. But the local authorities, right up to the Regional

Committee of the Communist Party, demanded immediate action to calm a restive populace. Moscow's patience was also wearing thin. The time was long overdue to bring this case to a close.

The fools confessed easily, and willingly signed candid admissions of guilt, but in rather idiosyncratic fashion. One day they would confess to something, while the next day they would deny it. And if they did not deny it, then they invariably got the details all wrong. One time they would forget the murder site, another time mouth utter nonsense about the victim's appearance. Or they would err in describing a victim's age and dress. But then, so what—they were fools! That is, mentally retarded. They could expect to be confused.

The fools were interrogated and taken to the crime scenes. The murders still continued. In September 1983 an unidentified woman's corpse was found in a shelterbelt on the outskirts of Novoshakhtinsk. In October the body of Vera Shevkun turned up in the woods near a cotton factory in Shakhty. In December the body of Seryozha Markov, with more than seventy knife wounds in it, was discovered near the suburban platform of Persianovka. At the time the fools were being held in jail cells.

Still, the criminal investigation bureau, defending its theory while adding creative embellishment to it, came to the conclusion that the band of maniacs had not been completely rendered harmless. That is, part of the band was behind bars but the other members, cleverly removing suspicion from their jailed compatriots, continued their sordid activities.

M. Tyapkin and A. Ponomarev, both mentally defective, were arrested in connection with the case of Shevkun and Markov. Both were fellow students of Kalenik. Had they killed? Of course! With a knife? What else? More wholehearted confessions followed.

But so did the killings. On January 10, 1984, the disfigured corpse of Natalya Shalopinina—that same girl who a year earlier had accompanied her friend Olga Kuprinato the bus station, herself to die soon afterward in unknown circumstances—was found in Aviators' Park. On February 22, the corpse of Marta Ryabenko, minus nipples and uterus, was discovered in the same park.

And on February 26, in the same park again, N. Beskorsy, an invalid from childhood and mentally retarded, was caught redhanded while clumsily attempting rape. After a few days of questioning, Beskorsy claimed responsibility for the rapes and murders of Shalopinina and Ryabenko.

According to the way the police saw it, the band of maniacs had increased in number. This was no longer a boarding school for mentally retarded children, but a regular den of thieves, a hotbed of crime. The number of deranged maniacs in the city of Rostov was much more than local psychiatrists had imagined.

The case continued to grow. Twenty-three murders by October 1984. In 1984 alone there were eleven murders. Later it turned out there were fifteen. This was Chikatilo's peak activity, a time when his passions ran rampant.

Meanwhile the fools, each and every one of them, continued to give testimony, confirming yesterday's denials and vice versa. The absurdity of their depositions sticks out like a sore thumb in the case materials. Issa Kostoev's team, after the case had been turned over to them, instantly turned up any number of enigmatic details. For example, the same organ cut out of the same victim turned up in three different places, all of them rather far from one another.

The fools, in spite of promptings, got mixed up in their answers and in turn confused the investigators. The latter became the prisoners and victims of their own methods. It is now being said that force was used against the fools to influence their testimony. We cannot say for sure, but certainly they were not treated with kid gloves. One died during the investigation, another attempted suicide.

"There was no need to pressure these people," said Amurkhan Yandiev. "The detectives had already gotten everything out of them that they needed. But how could the investigators have believed the testimony of these mentally ill individuals?"

Maybe they did not believe them all that much, but the authorities—meaning the Regional Committee of the Communist Party—still preferred their theory of a gang of madmen. The year was 1984 when all this was happening, a time when one frail leader, Konstantin Chernenko, replaced another, Yuri Andropov. Perestroika was still several long months away, and the Communist Party wielded absolute power over every facet of life. It knew better how to run the factories and plow the fields, how to develop culture and render justice. The party knew a criminal from an innocent person when it saw one.

As far as the professionals were concerned, they harbored serious doubts, whether they belonged to the party or not, about a gang of mentally retarded sex maniacs. Not only did Vladimir Kazakov, head of the investigative team from Moscow, doubt it—he rejected the theory outright. It really was nonsense: here were the suspects behind bars, and yet there was no end in sight to the killings. Only in fall of the following year, when the word "perestroika" began to circulate in everyday speech and the investigation was taken in hand by Issa Kostoyev, were the fools allowed to go free.

Their release did not come easy for Kostoyev. Perestroika had not changed the mentality of the local powers. Perestroika was something that happened far away, in Moscow or Leningrad, but not here. The fate of these innocents was not decided by logical arguments in their defense, or by appeals to the law, but by Kostoyev's good relations with then Prosecutor General of the country, Rekunkov. To the proponents of the version of the fools, Kostoyev basically said, "Stop behaving like idiots. You're lucky it's not you in jail instead of them."

It would be naive to think that all the investigators working in the prosecutor's office were obsessed with the group of boarding school graduates. There were those who set out on different paths. In such a multilayered case there are bound to be offshoots. Kazakov, for example, tried a different tack. On November 20, 1984, he sent a letter to the chief physician of the Rostov dermatology and venereal diseases clinic, asking for a list of all males residing in the area who had recently visited the clinic for treatment or who had complained of sexual dysfunction.

There were perfectly good reasons for writing such a letter. Forensic analysis had turned up the presence of crab lice on the corpse of seventeen-year-old Natalia Shalopinina, who had been brutally murdered in Aviators' Park on January 9, 1984. Her rapist and murderer should most likely have contracted them as well. If so, then sooner or later—and more likely sooner due to the overwhelming need to itch such lice produce—he would see a doctor. And any doctor, in turn, would refer the patient to the clinic.

Kazakov was on the right track. His line of reasoning should have led investigators to the true killer. Instead, it turned up nothing.

Approximately half an hour after Shalopinina's murder, Chikatilo left the park and took a bus to Shakhty. The day was almost over, and it was time to get back to his family. It is possible that he already began to feel an unbearable itch that evening. In any event, before reaching home, he stopped in at a pharmacy on Engels Street where the pharmacist, an elderly woman, gave him mercury ointment and told

him how to apply it. He never showed up at the
Rostov clinic for venereal diseases.

Eight years later, Chikatilo would vehemently
deny at the trial that he ever had the infection or had
ever used any ointment. He made it sound as if this
was more shameful and much worse than any of the
crimes he had been charged with.

Insofar as the sex-crazed killer—or killers—went
after young boys as well as girls and women, the
police had to check out the relatively small gay community. As a social class in the Soviet Union, homosexuals occupied a rung even lower than that of
prostitutes and vagrants. Even today, homosexual
acts between consenting adults is considered a crime.
Anyone who exhibited even the slightest tendency to
homoerotic love was called in for questioning. It produced another dead end.

Still one more theory was that the killer might
own an automobile, which was a fairly rare occurrence in Soviet Russia, or work as a driver for a factory. The reason behind this was that the victims had
been found scattered over a wide radius. Some of
them had been discovered miles away from the
nearest bus or train stop. One victim was even more
than seventy-five miles away from where it was supposed she had disappeared. The investigators had no
idea then—and they probably would not have
believed it—that some of Chikatilo's victims willingly followed him over long distances to their
deaths. Thus, any person holding a driver's license or
who used a vehicle in connection with his job was

checked. More than 150,000 individuals who fit the description were checked before this line of inquiry was abandoned.

Overall, close to half a million people, almost ten percent of the entire population of the Rostov region, was checked in connection with Operation Shelterbelt. The results, however, were not entirely futile. As a result of these checks, the Rostov police solved more than 1,000 cases, many of them involving aggravated assault and murder.

But the one they were looking for, the real Shelterbelt killer, escaped their dragnet.

CHAPTER 7

Interview with the Man in the Cage

SUMMER 1992

WE SUCCEEDED in arranging our interview with the alleged murderer many months before sentencing. The Rostov Regional Court had already heard the case about the fifty-three sexually motivated, savage killings.

By then, most of the people following the trial had no doubt who the real killer was. Reporters assigned to the case obviously felt the same way: words like "murderer," "maniac," and "monster" dotted newspaper headlines.

Still, neither the prosecution nor the defense had begun its summation. And the judge had yet to pronounce the word "murderer." Doctors had ruled Chikatilo competent to stand trial, and responsible for his actions. His family had been removed from Rostov province under an assumed name for fear of retaliation by the relatives of the victims.

While no one entering the courtroom had their bags searched or their documents checked, the probable killer was guarded with extreme caution. Contrary to normal procedure, he was held in a rather decent—by Russian standards—two-person KGB isolation cell. He could read newspapers and listen to the radio. However, a face-to-face meeting with him was impossible.

Before court was called to order, Judge Akubzhanov sometimes allowed photojournalists to take a few pictures of the stooping man in the cage, who acted as if he wasn't even aware of their flashbulbs. Yet, when entering his cage, he always looked quickly around the courtroom to see if the members of the press correspondents were in their front row seats.

We submitted written questions and received his short answers scribbled in a jerky hand. Sometimes letters and punctuation were missing, as if he were in a hurry, as if he weren't spending long and solitary evenings in his cell. His rambling replies were full of incomplete sentences, repetitions, and empty phrases.

Amazingly, he had absolutely nothing to say. He was an average Soviet citizen, no different from anyone else. He had been a teacher and a supply clerk. He read newspapers, listened to the radio, watched television. He was a father, husband, and grandfather.

Because Chikatilo had still not been convicted of murder, we were barred from asking him point-blank:

Did you kill? Did you truly have an irresistible
attraction for young girls and boys? What did you feel
when you were seeking a victim? When you were
killing? Any answer to such questions could be used
against him. We were not sympathetic toward the
defendant, but the twisted history of the case made
us cautious. We could not ask him, for example, any
questions having any connection with the details of
the crimes, the investigation or the trial itself.
Therefore, we limited ourselves to asking Chikatilo
questions that dealt with his life prior to his arrest.
Here are excerpts from that interview. These are his
exact words. Nothing has been changed. The only
editing done has been to shorten the material for
space considerations.

Q: What events from your childhood, in your
opinion, had the most influence on shaping your personality?
A: We lived in occupied territories from 1941-1943.
After battles we gathered the corpses, in pieces and
covered in blood. I saw blown-apart children on the
streets . . . bullets, explosions, fires, burning huts.

   Famines caused by Stalin. In 1933, according to
the stories my mother and father told, my older
brother Stepan was kidnapped and eaten. My parents
always warned me not to go anywhere alone. We hid
in basements.

   Cold and hunger were constant in my childhood. I
nearly died of hunger lying in the tall weeds.

My father, a partisan commandeer, was captured by the Germans, liberated by the Americans. He was repressed, worked in the Komi forests. When he got out he was tubercular, coughed up blood.

Q: What are your political convictions?

A: I was a member of the Communist Party for 25 years. I graduated from four universities of Marxism-Leninism. I was an ardent fighter for the triumph of communism around the world.

I am very much distressed by the fact that I wasted my whole life on utopian ideals that had nothing to do with reality. The collapse of communism was a personal tragedy, a blow to my beliefs.

Q: How did you bring up your children?

A: My wife and I raised two children. They are hard workers, modest. We did not spoil them, my wife and I worked 40 years for the good of the country. We didn't live in luxury and we taught our children the value of an honest day's work.

Q: Do you believe in God and the immortality of the soul?

A: While the war was raging and my father was at the front, and then in captivity, then disappeared without a trace, and we were dying from cold and hunger, I always prayed to God and turned to Him as my mother had taught me. And God always helped me.

I don't picture God as some elderly being but as a higher source, Universal Intellect. It is our Creator, our Guardian, a higher Authority that safeguards all of us from disease and misfortune.

Another influence came from my study of atheism, which was the main subject taught at the four universities of Marxism-Leninism I attended. This caused a split in my thinking. Now, when I listen to sermons and prayers, I pray myself. And I believe in the immortality of the soul.

Q: For whom do you feel special gratitude?

A: For my wife. I love her, admire her. I am grateful for the fact that she tolerated my sexual impotency— we really had no real intercourse, just imitation. She suffered because of this, because of my character and helplessness. But she defended me whenever anyone tormented me at work.

Q: You once stated that you are more woman than man. How does that manifest itself?

A: During childhood I spent more time with female friends. Even now I relate better to women. I have trouble finding common topics of interest with men.

When I was a child, boys became attached to me as if I were a girl. It was the same in the army and later in prison, and on business trips. The upshot is I no longer know which sex I relate to more. It's a kind of dichotomy. I like the attentions of men.

Q: Did you have close friends?

A: No, I didn't have a close friend. I'm alone in my daydreams, in my fantasies. In my resentment against injustice.

Q: How do you prefer to relax? Where did you normally spend vacations?

A: I never took a vacation anywhere for the whole forty years I worked. I don't like holidays, I can't stand idleness. All my time off was spent puttering about the house.

Q: You have said more than once that you are a victim of society. Can you explain what you mean?

A: The meaning of life is to leave some trace behind on earth. Whether I was working, studying, or creating—I gave my all to it until the desire was taken away from me. I was beaten about the hands and head. My business trips took me from my home, to railway stations and commuter trains. But I'm a domestic person, a country person. I love family, the hearth, children, grandchildren.

Because of my character—reserved, timid, shy, especially in childhood—I could not get adjusted to this society, I lived life my own way. I couldn't find answers to the questions about sex or family life that tormented me. Now these problems are being worked out, but in the past just the mention of them was considered a disgrace.

Q: What are your favorite books? And music?

A: When I was growing up all literature and music was devoted to the worldwide victory of communism. I was enthralled by military literature, especially books about partisans. I liked it because my father had been a commandeer of a partisan detachment. I especially liked revolutionary songs that exhorted us onward to the final triumph of communism. Back then literature and music weren't concerned with human relationships, or love and kindness.

Q: Would you change your life if you could return to the past, to about twenty years ago?

A: I dreamed of having a permanent job in one place, of living in the country and having more children. My tragedy is that I did not bear up against the pressures of contemporary urban civilization. I should have married earlier and gone to work somewhere in my village, without leaving home. The break from my family led to my being totally isolated from society.

Q: What do you consider to be the main traits of your personality? Are you outgoing or reserved?

A: Traits peculiar to me are candor, unbounded sincerity, goodness. Being reserved is an assumed trait, a direct influence of the aggressive environment that surrounds me.

CHAPTER 8

Face to Face with the Murderer

SEPTEMBER 1984

NINETEEN HUNDRED eighty four was a terrible year: there were fifteen murders from January through September. The summer of 1984 was the worst: eleven of the fifteen murders took place during that period.

The Rostov criminal investigation bureau was on the verge of despair. There were plenty of theories going around, but not one was reliable. The "case of the fools" was in full swing. Shaburov, Kalenik, Turov, Korzhov and the others willingly confessed to everything, yet their testimony was coming apart at the seams. It was doubtful that any of the more experienced investigators took them seriously. More likely than not, the police went along with it to hide the fact that they had been unable to pick up the trail of the murderer after so many years.

But whom to look for, and how? The only reliable clue was the sperm found on the bodies and clothing of the victims. Analysis determined that it belonged to the least common type. Its rarity, however, is relative: one out of every ten men in Europe has this type.

In the summer of 1984, Viktor V. Burakov turned to psychiatrists and sexual pathologists for help. It was the first time in the history of the case that experts in human deviant behavior were consulted. Burakov rounded up all the leading specialists from the department of psychiatry at the Rostov Medical Institute and asked them to become familiar with the case. Then he asked them to create a profile of the murderer—or profiles, if there were more than one.

The specialists became acquainted with the case and refused on the basis of insufficient information. The only one who agreed to help was Assistant Professor Aleksandr O. Bukhanovsky. He made a suggestion about which angle to take when approaching the problem.

Nowadays the role of Dr. Bukhanovsky in tracking down the Rostov serial killer is either rejected outright or recognized as having been the most decisive. The truth lies somewhere in the middle. Dr. Bukhanovsky was the only physician who agreed to help the investigation. His involvement resulted in the first profile of the killer.

What was known about the man before that? He was a man 25 to 50 years old, 5'10" tall, give or take a few inches; his shoe size was no less than 10. His sperm was of the least common type. That was the extent of the profile.

Bukhanovsky's contribution was that the killer, in his opinion, was not only prone to sexual perversities—the pedophilia, necrophilia, homosexualism and sadism left no doubt of that—but that, to all appearances, he also suffered from sexual inadequacies. It was highly probable that he vented his impotency on his victims, as if trying to compensate for what nature had denied him. It should be recalled that investigator Kazakov, in his letter to dermatological-venereal clinics, was not only looking for a man who had contracted crab lice from his victim, but for anyone who had seen a doctor to complain of a "lack of attraction toward women, or an inability to consummate intercourse."

This information added something essential to the rather weak profile of the killer. Although the number of men suffering from some degree of sexual impotency is quite large, it is nonetheless modest when compared to the group of men aged 25 to 50 and 5'8" to 6'0' feet tall. When these two groups intersect, the numbers are significantly reduced, especially when a blood or sperm analysis is included.

The police now had something to go on. However, there was only one way to make use of this information, and that was to eliminate as many people as possible. That meant checking thousands, if not tens of thousands, of men.

Though it cost him a great deal of effort, Viktor Burakov was able to get constant police detachments concentrated in the Rostov province, especially in the cities as Rostov, Shakhty, Novoshakhtinsk, and Novocherkassk. The investigations centered on those places where large numbers of people congregated—bus stations, for example.

Still, Burakov simply did not have the manpower to go around, so reinforcements had to be brought in from the regional police departments. That was how District Inspector Captain Aleksandr A. Zanosovsky from the Pervomaisky police department in Rostov joined forces with the investigative team of Operation Shelterbelt in the summer of 1984. Zanosovsky was assigned to the case in August. His objective was the suburban bus station, which he knew like the back of his hand.

The station now attracted the attention of the search brigade, and not just because thousands of people passed through it daily. There were other reasons that warranted taking a closer look. Detectives already knew that Natalya Shalopinina, killed in January, had checked her belongings here. From a token discovered near her corpse, the police were able to retrieve her briefcase. It contained, among other things, a photo i.d. card, which allowed them to establish the corpse rather quickly. Moreover, the brigade knew that another Natalya—Golosovskaya—had hoped to make her way to Novoshakhtinsk, and the best way would have been by bus from this very terminal.

Zanosovsky began the stakeout in his usual manner. This consisted of walking around without drawing attention to himself. He kept an eye out for anyone exhibiting any unprovoked signs of anxiety or distress, or anything else that might be regarded as suspicious. The captain knew from experience to focus on rash movements, unkempt dress or unusual baggage—on anything not in keeping with the local customs and manners. Drunks had to be checked out, too, even though the excessive use of alcohol within the confines of the Rostov region could hardly be considered a phenomenon out of the ordinary.

Captain Zanosovsky also kept in mind that the "Shelterbelt" killer preyed upon boys, girls and young women. About an hour before he would go off duty, his legs ached and his eyes were bloodshot from watching the endless stream of old men and women, young couples, and hordes of shrieking boys and girls beginning their annual September trek back to school. His head rang from the buzz of voices and public address announcements, the roar of diesel engines, the shouting matches near the ticket windows, and the shuffling of feet.

But something caught his attention. It was a middle-aged man wearing glasses, properly attired in a gray jacket and tie, and holding a briefcase. There are always many such travelers at these stations, bustling about or killing time by casually strolling back and forth, or burying their noses in newspapers.

But Zanosovsky detected something unusual about this one's behavior. He appeared to be walking around without any specific goal. His movements would abruptly change, as if he were shifting gears from one speed to another. A young girl in a pale-colored dress entered his field of vision, and he literally swooped down upon her, uttered something and then stood there, his mouth partially open, in anticipation of her answer. He cut her off and began talking without interruption, smiling now, his eyes lit up.

Maybe it meant nothing at all, Zanosovsky thought to himself. The man had met his daughter, or niece, or a friend of his daughter. She was bashful and didn't know what to say—after all, a big age difference separated them. The man was just passing the time before his bus arrived.

Nothing special happened, so Zanosovsky continued his beat. He walked out onto the platform, went back inside, stood awhile near the ticket counter, and for the hundredth—maybe even thousandth—time checked out the endless lines. He strode past a newspaper stand, pharmaceutical booth, cafeteria, and walked up and down the aisles between the seats. The man with the briefcase was still haranguing the girl.

Zanosovsky couldn't rid himself of the notion that the man with the briefcase was behaving strangely. People of that stature don't attach themselves like that to young girls they don't know, and they certainly don't try to pressure the ones they do know. For the whole time he had been talking to her, the girl tried to avoid his gaze. If they knew each other, she would not be acting that way. She was not bashful, but visibly disturbed, and didn't seem to know what to say.

She suddenly stood up and, without saying goodbye or looking at the man, walked out onto the platform. The captain watched her until she boarded a bus.

The gleam in the bespectacled man's eyes dimmed as soon as she had turned her back on him. For a minute or two he sat in a chair, then abruptly stood up and again began pacing back and forth around the hall, his eyes darting left and right.

Zanosovsky already knew what the man was looking for.

Several times, after spotting a young girl by herself, he would quickly approach her, as if suddenly coming across an old acquaintance, and attempt to start up a conversation. From a distance it might appear that he had made mistaken the girl for somebody else. Each time the girl would say something that obviously was not what the man wanted to hear. Clearly disappointed, he would immediately back off.

Zanosovsky glanced at his watch. In just a few minutes his shift would end. Either he had to check out this man right now, or let him continue his strolls around the station. He didn't look like a criminal—just a persistent flirt in spite of his meek appearance.

"Excuse me, comrade."

The inspector touched the man on his sleeve. The man froze, casting a frightened look at the policemen.

"District Inspector Captain Zanosovsky. Your documents, please." Soviet citizens must always carry their travel papers.

"Why? What's wrong?" The man was clearly agitated, even afraid. His voice registered displeasure even as he tried to sound ingratiating.

"I just want to check your documents. Do you have your passport? Let me see it, please."

"Okay, okay, just a minute. . ."

The man shifted the briefcase from one hand to the other. He squeezed the handle so hard that his knuckles turned completely white. The captain took mental note of this.

The man fumbled in his jacket pocket, pulled out his wallet, and began to flip through various bills and receipts. He suddenly became talkative.

"Here is my passport, my identification card, business pass. I just came back from a business trip, and I'm on my way home. I'm just trying to kill some time until the bus comes."

He winked conspiratorially at the captain. Then he became silent, breathing heavily.

His documents were in complete order. Zanosovsky studied them carefully, returned them to the man, apologized for the inconvenience and saluted. He was in uniform, and regulations required that he be courteous to everyone he addressed, including suspicious-looking characters in bus stations who were hitting on young girls.

"Everything is in order. Sorry to have troubled you," said the captain. "Have a good trip."

The man quickly put away his documents, nodded and beat a hasty retreat from the captain, whose shift had just come to an end. Zanosovsky headed for home, muttering under his breath the man's rather unusual name—Chikatilo. There was something strange about his behavior.

★ ★ ★

Two weeks passed. Thursday, the 13th of September, was destined to become a memorable day in the history of Operation Shelterbelt. On that day Chikatilo was arrested and put behind bars.

He was tried three months later—but not for murder! Instead, Chikatilo was accused of petty theft, the details of which will be explained later, and let go.

He remained a free man until November 1990. During these six years he killed twenty-one more times.

★ ★ ★

On September 13th, 1984, Captain Aleksandr Zanosovsky was making his rounds of the suburban bus station. He had done this so many times he had lost count. This time he had a partner along, Sheik-Akhmed Akhmatkhanov, also from the Pervomaisky police department. Both were in their street clothes.

As the day was drawing to an end, Zanosovsky spotted a tall bespectacled man, the same one whose documents he had checked two weeks before—the same one who had been so nervous when asked to show his passport.

In the intervening time, the captain had seen many faces and checked many documents, but he instantly remembered this face as soon as he saw it. He took a closer look. Just like the previous time, Zanosovsky noticed, the tall man was walking around the hall, looking other passengers in the eyes. It might have seemed to a casual observer that the man was simply killing time, but there was something about his behavior that suggested otherwise. Zanosovsky again had the feeling that this one bore closer watching. He told his partner not to let the man out of his sight.

Akhmatkhanov was also surprised at how closely the tall man wearing glasses resembled the crumpled and torn police sketch he had been carrying around in his pocket. The sketch had always seemed lifeless before, more a diagram or an approximation of a person than a portrait. It would take a good imagination, a detective's sixth sense, to see the similarity, but Akhmatkhanov spotted it.

As bad luck would have it, Akhmatkhanov showed up for work that day in a bright yellow shirt which could be seen from far away. It was like a beacon shining through the station. Fearing the shirt would draw attention, Zanosovsky suggested they split up. He would concentrate on the man with the briefcase, although he would have preferred to keep a greater distance. What if the man suddenly remembered him as the one who had checked his docu-

At the beginning of the trial, Chikatilo identifies the "source of his troubles," as he holds up a copy of the newspaper *Sobesednik*, which features photos of naked girls.

Chikatilo being led out of the courthouse.

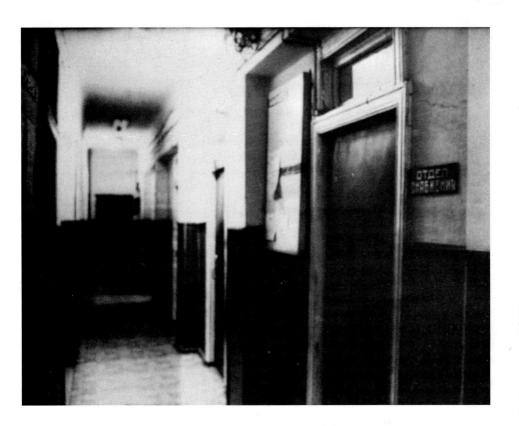

Supply department of the State industrial association
"Rostovnerud" in Rostov where Andrei Chikatilo
worked from 1981–1984.

Above: Aviators' Park in Rostov-on-Don. Chikatilo killed seven people in this park.

Below: Drug store on the main street of Rostov-on-Don where Chikatilo bought an ointment against crab lice.

For the protection of all involved, a cage was installed in the courtroom to hold Chikatilo during the trial.

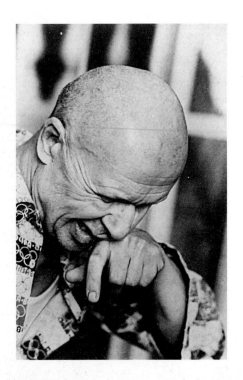

Chikatilo inside his cage.
He wore the same shirt,
a souvenir from the 1980
Summer Olympics
in Moscow, throughout
the trial.

Above: A flat (belonging to "Rostovnerud") where Chikatilo lived for a while.

Below: Shakhty vocational training school, where Chikatilo worked as an educator and a foreman from 1978–1980.

ments? Akhmatkhanov's job was to keep his eyes glued on anyone who came into contact with the man.

The man wandered a bit more around the station. Apparently he didn't see anyone that caught his eye, for soon after he walked out on to the platform and boarded a bus heading in the direction of the airport. Zanosovsky and Akhmatkhanov took off in pursuit. After two or three stops the man with the briefcase suddenly got off the bus, crossed the street and hopped a trolleybus going back toward the city.

For at least two hours he weaved back and forth, changing buses and trolleys. As evening wore on, he continued to make illogical zigs and zags, all the while taking advantage of every opportunity to engage unknown women and girls in conversation. But his attempts were clumsy and unsuccessful. He was constantly looking around, and over his shoulder.

As the detectives continued their surveillance, Akhmatkhanov suggested that their "client" sensed he was being tailed. But Zanosovsky was sure of himself. He had gained a lot of experience over the years from tailing Rostov's infamous pickpockets, a wily and cautious bunch. They were professionals who could feel someone behind their backs, without letting on that they knew they were being followed— not like this jittery amateur.

This time, though, the detectives had overestimated their ability to blend in with the surroundings. Akhmatkhanov's loud yellow shirt might have given them away. In any event, the man with the brown briefcase continued to bounce around the city, trying to erase his tracks and confuse his followers. Only when it seemed to him that he had thrown his trackers off the scent did his former confidence return.

In the center of town, on Engels Street, he squeezed his way through a crowded bus to a tall, blond girl. He began to stare at her cleavage. When the girl caught him looking, she quickly jumped out at the next stop.

At this time of day the bus was packed. Hemmed in by the other passengers next to a magnificent-looking woman, the man could not control himself and placed his hand on her thigh. Unlike the girl before, the woman loudly proclaimed what she thought of the man and what ought to be done with such sons of bitches. Now it was his turn to make a quick getaway. Zanosovsky and Akhmatkhanov barely made it off the bus after him.

Crowds lined the sidewalks at the intersection of Engels Street and Voroshilovsky Avenue. After a day spent working and standing on lines, people wanted to forget their cares for awhile and relax by doing some window-shopping. For awhile the man actually seemed to forget about his troubles and strolled around downtown completely carefree. Despite the time and the effort already expended in pursuit of the man, the two detectives were dead set upon carrying out their surveillance of the man until they could find the right pretext to drag him into the nearest precinct.

Zanosovsky decided to take his time—he had already stopped Chikatilo once and had been obliged to let him go. He was afraid the same thing would happen again. After all, this lanky character had not done anything that would warrant a trip to the police station. It might be considered offensive to look down someone's dress, but it was not against the law. If the man produced his impeccable documents a second time and gave a plausible explanation for his wanderings about town, the detective would have no alternative but to apologize again. Any person can spend his free time as he or she chooses. That includes getting acquainted with girls, regardless of their age.

Zanosovsky and Akhmatkhanov continued in pursuit of their target, who now dropped in on some of Rostov's sleazier joints. In the "Central" restaurant he struck up a conversation with some slightly intoxicated women in short skirts. They shared a few laughs with the man, and asked him for cigarettes, but when their boyfriends appeared, the man had to back off.

He crossed the avenue and walked into an establishment that served cocktails on the second floor. The detectives waited for him outside. He came out soon after, as sober as he went in, and clearly disappointed. Slowly he made his way past the store windows toward Gorky Park. He sat down on a bench under a tree. He sat there a long time, then suddenly got up and headed for the train station. There he stood silently alongside a sleeping woman for about twenty minutes. He eventually grew tired of looking at her and wandered away. After looking around and not finding anyone else worthy of attention, he left the train station and crossed the square to the main bus station. He made a few rounds on the first and second floors, where he found another young girl.

She was obviously in no mood to deal with this stranger. Without even bothering to hear him out, she abruptly rose from her seat and moved to another. Captain Zanosovsky felt that now was the time to take action. Trying to pick up women in public places might be unbecoming—even indecent— behavior, but nothing more. Moreover, the Shelterbelt criminal did not necessarily meet his victims at railway stations or on crowded streets. That was only one theory, and maybe not even the leading one. As long as the man with the briefcase kept getting turned down left and right, there was technically no reason for the police to intervene. But what if the next girl were to strike up a conversation with him and get propositioned? What kind of proposition would it be? Would it lead to a wooded area, or to the nearest park?

Zanosovsky approached the girl who had moved away from the stranger and, for the first time that evening, revealed his identity. He didn't explain anything, just asked: *What did that man want to talk about? Nothing in particular. Nonsense.* Then the captain asked her: *If he comes this way again, don't*

*turn him down. Agree to whatever he says. Go wher-
ever he orders, and don't be afraid—we'll be right
behind you the whole time.* To his surprise, the girl
agreed.

The trap was set, the bait was laid. But the
stranger didn't return. Instead, he sat down in a far
corner of the station. Settled into a leather chair, he
closed his eyes and began dozing.

Zanosovsky and Akhmatkhanov were in desperate need of sleep themselves. But they didn't dare,
not even in turns. For a good two hours they kept
their eyes peeled on the man, who was sleeping like a
baby. He always slept well, whether at home in his
own bed, or at work at his desk after being out all
night during one of his nocturnal adventures, or on
his prison cot. He never had a problem with eating or
sleeping.

It was after two in the morning when the man
opened his eyes. He stretched, yawned and rose from
his seat. His nap had apparently renewed his
strength, for once again he began to circle the station.

His attention was caught by a family of four—
father, mother, and two stout and sturdy daughters—
sprawled out on benches in a corner. With all their
bundles and suitcase, they were obviously traveling
somewhere. All were sound asleep.

What had caught his eye was the hiked-up skirt
on one of the daughters, revealing pink thighs and
lace panties. The man stared unashamedly, breathing
heavily through his nose. He adjusted his glasses to
get a better look. The father cocked open an eye and

looked at the stranger quizzically until he figured out
what had lured him here. Without fully waking, he
silently smoothed out his daughter's skirt and went
right back to sleep. The man shrugged and set off in
hot pursuit of other such unexpected pleasures.

It was now three o'clock in the morning. The
policemen felt a chill in their bones from the brisk
predawn air and the long, sleepless night. They could
barely keep their eyes open. The stranger, sagging
from his run of bad luck, again settled himself in a
chair and stared vacantly over the heads of the
sleeping travelers. He was close to drifting off, too.

His face eyes suddenly became animated. He sat
up in his chair and even leaned forward a bit. A new
girl was coming right toward him, wiggling her hips.
She was poorly dressed, dirty, thickly made up and
quite buxom. She sat down next to him. She seemed
to crave company as much as he did. They immediately struck up a conversation. Not even five minutes had elapsed before the girl moved closer to him.
She reeked of sweat and cheap perfume. The man
found her scent pleasing.

He grabbed hold of her shoulders and brought her
closer to him. A wave of desire slowly welled up
inside him. The main thing now was not to lose it.
Slowly, carefully, he squeezed her a little tighter and
tried to roll her over on top of him. The girl didn't
resist but she didn't respond to his movements,
either. She could have been on drugs, or had too
much to drink.

She lay her head on his knee, apparently dozing. He covered her head and chest with his jacket, arranged his briefcase in such a way as to serve as barrier, and took a look around.

Zanosovsky and Akhmatkhanov observed the couple from behind newspapers.

The man looked around once again, assumed an air of nonchalance, and furtively stuck his hand under his jacket. His eyes rolled back in pleasure.

His hand stole along the girl's neck to her chest. Finding an opening at the top of her dress, his fingers groped for the hollow between her breasts. With a bit of doing, they made their way under the synthetic fabric of her bra to the soft flesh beneath.

That was as far as he could go for now. Not enough. How he would have loved to rip the girl's clothes off and bury his face between her breasts. But that would have to wait for later.

The girl said something to him, but he could not concentrate on her words. He was too aroused. They seemed to be arguing—as if she were telling him not to touch her in public, while he protested and tried to reassure her that everything was alright.

Slowly, unwillingly, he took his hand out from under her dress, placed it on his briefcase and neatly folded his jacket. For a few minutes more she lay on his knees, then sat up lazily, stretching and yawning. They seemed to be making plans to meet again.

After they descended the stairs to the first floor and went into their respective bathrooms to freshen up, they parted in opposite directions.

It was now five o'clock. In keeping with his assignment, Akhmatkhanov started after the girl, but Zanosovsky gestured to let her go. There was no point. He had enough of walking around in circles—the time to take the man was now.

No longer bothering to conceal themselves, they occupied the seat right behind the man in the first streetcar of the morning. They got off with him at Budenny Avenue in the center of town. He headed toward the market. The detectives openly followed him, keeping just a few steps behind.

In another minute or two it would all be over. They'd pronounce the usual phrases and suggest that the man follow them quietly down to the police station. He would agree—what else could he do?

A few years later Chikatilo would say, "On September 13th, 1984, the man who had checked my documents earlier in the new bus station in Rostov-on-Don, followed me, concealing himself behind a newspaper, and then apprehended me at the Central Market. He was with someone else. Apparently, they had been following me and had seen how I began talking with one girl and then another. They also saw how one of them had slept on my knees with her breasts exposed, and how I had touched them. When I got up and left with her from this station, I noticed that they also got up and came after me. The girl, evidently, went somewhere, and I went to the Central Market where they arrested me."

Chikatilo has an excellent memory and a sharp eye. But one wonders why, if he knew he was being followed, he did not attempt to make a quiet and undetectable getaway rather than continuing to approach girls on the street and in the stations. Why didn't he hide behind his usual mask of a meek and upright citizen? Couldn't he tame his lust, especially in front of the police? Did he believe in his invulnerability before the law, or did he count upon his "black hood" to protect him? Or maybe—and with good reason—he counted upon the red card he was carrying that identified him as a freelance employee of the Department of Internal Affairs, or upon other documents, KGB papers, still locked away in an official safe somewhere, far from the eyes of the uninitiated?

In front of the market, Captain Aleksandr Zanosovsky quickened his pace, caught up with the tall bespectacled man and said softly behind his back, "Your documents, citizen!"

The man turned around and recognized the policeman who had checked his identity two weeks ago. He froze.

"Your documents!" repeated Zanosovsky, louder this time.

Beads of perspiration instantly and profusely broke out on the man's face. "Never in my life have I seen such sweat pour off a person," Zanosovsky said later. "It was literally rolling off him."

Horror was written on the man's sweat-soaked and suddenly pitiful face. Not quite certain what he was doing, he opened his briefcase with trembling hands, rummaged about, and extended dark red Soviet passport to the captain.

Zanosovsky took a quick glance at the photograph, then at the man's face. He flipped through the pages of his passport, held together by a paper clip.

Registered in the city of Shakhty; married with two children; nationality—Ukrainian; place of birth—Sumskaya province; year of birth—1936.

Name: Andrei Romanovich Chikatilo.

PART II

Andrei Chikatilo— An Ordinary Life

CHAPTER 9

Childhood, Adolescence, Youth

1936-1970

"I WAS BORN October 16, 1936, in the village of Yablochnoye, Akhtyrsky region, Sumskaya province. My parents were hungry and I, too, went hungry until I was twelve, when I ate bread for the first time in my life. My father and mother almost died from hunger in 1933-34. In 1933 they lost their older son, and my brother, Stepan, who was kidnapped by desperately starving people and eaten." These words are taken verbatim from Chikatilo's autobiography, compiled during the investigation.

Russia has known so many calamities in this century that it becomes extremely difficult, even with the help of official documents and other written materials, to accurately recreate a person's childhood, even if it was lived just a few decades ago. It becomes especially difficult if the person grew up in those parts of the country that were exposed to one war after another, and all the consequences that follow.

141

Chikatilo's parents passed away at the end of the 1980s. The family had long since moved from Yablochnoye, and very few people still living there remember them. Therefore, the reader has to believe Chikatilo's own words. Of course, certain events may have been confused, exaggerated, forgotten, or deliberately omitted.

Chikatilo gave a rather grandiose title to his life story: "A Biography of the Defendant A.R. Chikatilo, Citizen of the USSR, Victim of Famine and Cannibalism in 1933 and 1947, Stalinist Repressions, Stagnation and the Crisis of Perestroika."

Three characteristic features of the author's personality are reflected in the title: his predilection for bombast; his political convictions as a long-time Communist Party member; and his desire to embellish his own background. His autobiography presents certain details of his background which, if they do not justify his crimes, then at least try to put an objective spin on their evil nature.

One example is the often-repeated and tragic history of his unfortunate older brother Stepan. During the terrible Ukrainian famine in the early 1930s, there truly were instances of cannibalism. Such cases are historically documented and were openly discussed in the post-Stalin era press, even more so during perestroika. Andrei Chikatilo was an avid reader of newspapers.

It is not surprising that a person who experienced such an unhappy childhood, whose older brother was allegedly killed and eaten, and who was warned not to leave the house on his own or he, too, might face the same fate, could have a damaged psyche later in life. If he eventually turned to criminal activities, he might point to various tragic details that led him astray. His rationale would be that, before he became a criminal, he was first a victim.

Having heard the version of the so-called cannibalized brother, investigators and journalists checked it out separately but came up empty-handed. There is no mention of a brother in any of the documents from that period, nor did any villagers from Yablochnoye have recollection of one. Whether he existed at all and, if he did, whether he really disappeared under such unusual circumstances, would be almost impossible to establish now with absolute certainty.

"From 1941 to 1944, I remember the horrors of my childhood years when we hid from bombings and shooting in cellars and open pits. We sat in ditches, hungry and cold, fleeing under the whistle of bullets. I remember our burning hut and the savagery of the fascists. In September of 1944, I went to school hungry and in tatters."

This much is believable. A country lad, living on occupied territories, does not need books or movies to teach him the brutal realities of war.

"1947-1948 was the height of the famine. Our bellies were all swollen from hunger. My sister and I ate grass or leaves.

"At school, I would collapse under the desk from hunger spells. I was dressed in rags. Other kids teased me, and I could not defend myself. I was too shy and timid. If I did not have any pens or ink, I would simply sit at my desk and cry. Sometimes the other students would tell the teacher, but all she would say was, 'Doesn't Andrei have a tongue of his own?' I was afraid to ask to go to the bathroom.

"I remember the horror of seeing bodies, starved to death, dragged along the streets, without coffins and wrapped in rags. I heard stories of cannibalism.

"But I stubbornly continued my studies, almost to the point of losing consciousness. I read many books. Learning did not come easily to me. My head often ached. And my attention span was not very good. Even now, I have trouble concentrating on things."

This last detail concerning his severe headaches is intriguing. It is obviously intended to bolster the theory that his mental illness can be traced to his early childhood. Further in his biography, he would cite another incident that involved injury to his head. Perhaps it is all true, but it is also possible that Chikatilo is laying the groundwork to blame his actions on the consequences of a traumatized psyche from childhood. On the other hand, it could be that he is simply grabbing at anything that might save his hide.

"I had trouble reading the blackboard—it was later diagnosed as congenital myopia. Now I wear glasses with a strong prescription. Back in school, I was afraid to ask what was written on the blackboard. I would get nervous and cry. There was nowhere to get glasses back then, and no one ever checked our vision. Later, when I was older, I was afraid of being called 'four-eyes.' I only began wearing glasses when I got married at the age of thirty.

"Since I could not learn my lessons in school, I studied extra hard at home on my own. That is how I came to be withdrawn, solitary, reclusive.

"When others teased me and called me 'skeleton,' or beat me, I would hide in our garden and wait until my mother returned home from work. I cried tears of shame and dreamed that my older brother Stepan would come and defend me. I was even ashamed of the fact that I was born.

"In 1949, I was thirteen years old and in the sixth grade. I remember, when I was home alone in our cold hut, how I would always get down on my knees before the icon in the corner and pray, 'Dear Lord, please bring back my father to me!' And in 1949 my father returned from the war. Sick with tuberculosis of the lungs, and spitting up blood, he would lay on the bed and moan. We needed bread on the table, but there wasn't any. My mother also complained of frequent headaches, but there was no treatment for her at the collective farm. People didn't know sickness in those days.

"During the war, my father was put in a foxhole without any weapons and told to wait until his comrade died—then he'd have his own rifle. He joined the partisans, killing the enemy wherever he met one. He was captured by the Germans, who put him to work in a mine. The Americans liberated him. After that, he was repressed, because, to Stalin's way of thinking, he could have been working for German and American intelligence. He was sent as a sick man to work in the logging areas in Komi and Chuvashia."

Everything in these lines is plausible and smacks of the truth. Such lives and fates are shared by literally hundreds of thousands of people in Russia. On the other hand, the portrait of Chikatilo's father is drawn somewhat schematically, as if taken from his beloved partisan literature and not from the heart. At times it seems that the legend about his father was made up recently, only after Chikatilo had been imprisoned. During the trial, the image of his father was also represented rather curiously, almost as if it had been lifted wholesale from some revolutionary slogan or banner: "My dad and I fought our whole lives for the triumph of communism around the world."

"1950. I tried to be better than all my classmates. I participated in literary and musical events, and I was the editor of our school newspaper. In 1951, I completed the seventh grade—that was as high as our school went. In the summer I worked on a collective farm. I wanted to enroll in a vocational school, but I was rejected because of my health. It was a very upsetting experience."

Chikatilo appears to be looking for pity with these lines. In fact, those former classmates of his who still remember him agree that he was physically strong. He somehow neglects to mention that their nickname for him was "Andrei the Strong."

"Eighth grade was offered in our area for the first time, and I attended our local school. I became a constant reader of *Pravda*.

"I worked the summer of 1952 in a brick factory on the farm. Once, part of a wall fell on me. I was bedridden at home for a long time.

"In 1953, it was announced during a meeting that Stalin had died. I cried and wanted to go to Moscow, but I didn't have any money. Back then, we were all very idealistic. We believed that communism would soon conquer the world. We were constantly marching through the streets, singing revolutionary songs.

"In the summer I worked on a state farm. In those days horse-drawn rakes were used for harvesting. Once, my horse became frightened and dragged me along the road. I fell on the iron rods of the rakes, bumping my head on the rocky road. As a result, I suffered a concussion.

"1954. I finished tenth grade, attending classes in an old and patched suit. There was a girl in my class, Lilya Barysheva, on whom I had a crush. I liked the way she played the role of a partisan fighter in one of our school performances. I also liked her modesty and femininity, and the freckles on her face. I didn't know what color her eyes were, because, with my poor vision, I was unable to look into them.

"One time, when we were at the movies, we sat so close to each other that our shoulders touched. We were hardly breathing. I was afraid our classmates would see us. I always wanted to talk to Lilya or visit her on my way home from school, but I never had the courage.

"Many boys and girls lived on our street. Sometimes, though not very often, I would join them. I was the only tenth-grader among all the kids in our village. All the others worked on the collective farm, or hung out and did nothing. I was considered brainy. I saw how the others played and rolled around in the grass, and how the boys used to pinch the girls.

"But I always dreamed of a different, more elevated, kind of love—like in the movies or novels. If a girl came and sat down next to me, I would act shy or afraid, and I wouldn't know what to say. All the other kids' parents pointed to me as an example: 'Look how quiet and modest Andrei is. He's in the tenth grade, and he still works at home and on the farm.' This used to drive me crazy—I was alone and alienated. I saw only one way out and that was to prove myself at school and work, while I waited for romance to come."

Chikatilo's former classmates and teachers from the Akhtyrskaya High School, as far as they can remember, agree that he was shy and withdrawn. As far as his noble love is concerned, it corresponds to the official style of the era in which he grew up: students were taught the difference between a love that is considered proper, and one that is depraved.

"Once, though, in the spring of 1954, I let my guard down. Tanya Bala, thirteen years old, came over to our house. She was wearing knickers under her dress. She asked for my sister, who wasn't home at the time. I told her that, but she didn't leave. That's when I pushed her down and lay on top of her. We were under some trees. We didn't take our clothes off, and I didn't touch her, but as soon as I lay down on her, I ejaculated.

"I was very upset by this weakness of mine, even though no one knew about it. After this unhappy event, I resolved to tame my sexual desires. I wrote down a vow: A 'cunt' is the organ of human reproduction. I swear never to touch anyone's but my wife's.' I hid my vow in a secret place."

This is the first and only time prior to his arrest, as far as we know, that Andrei used a four-letter word. But, either out of shame or hypocrisy, he wrote it in Latin letters, not Cyrillic. Afterward, he avoided such words altogether in any script.

"At the time I was reading a lot. My favorite books were ones about partisans, especially *The Young Guard*. I also used to draw up columns of numbers. One time I started to make a table of numbers, and I got almost as far as one million. In the eighth grade, I tried to make an atlas of all the provinces and regions. I knew the names of all the communist leaders."

Again, this is consistent with the times. All students had to memorize the names and faces of the leading communist figures, especially if they wanted to join the Komsomol, the Young Communist League. Later, any party member who sought permission to travel abroad was asked to name the leader of the communist party of Romania, Mongolia,

Uruguay, and so on. This was how a person's political reliability was determined.

There is one other detail in his biography that bears mentioning—Chikatilo's obsession with the partisan theme. It was in the role of partisan fighter that Lilya Barysheva captured his heart. He read more books on this subject in his spare time than any others. At every available chance, he brought up his father's partisan past. It may have been that he, too, secretly wished to be a member of this select group which combined the traits of restraint and recklessness, discipline and bravado.

The psychiatrists, sexual pathologists and psychologists who have examined Andrei Chikatilo, despite their differences of opinion concerning certain aspects of his life, all agree on one point: he should not be executed, even if justice demands it. This product of the communist system must be preserved and kept alive for further study.

It does not seem likely, however, that this will happen. Chikatilo has been judged mentally sound and responsible for his actions. The only possible outcome can be capital punishment.

Still, it is intriguing that the timid country boy, for all his talents and good intentions, somehow became a twentieth century version of Jack the Ripper.

To paraphrase a leading Moscow psychoanalyst who had the opportunity to observe him during the trial, Chikatilo was an exceptionally vulnerable, sensitive and nervous child. The difficulty he encountered in interacting with his peers, especially girls, and his fear of raising his hand to go to the bathroom, were linked to his poor self-esteem. He compensated for this by taking up unusual activities, like making columns of numbers, or memorizing the names of communist leaders. In his fantasies he pictured himself as the General Secretary of the Communist Party. The hostility he felt from his surroundings gave birth to a feeling of hatred, which grew over the years. Gradually, his inferiority complex, coupled with unsuccessful attempts at sex, were compensated for by a heightened interest in school, fascination with Marxist philosophy, and the hope of a quick communist triumph that would symbolically rid the world of the injustice and hostility he perceived.

Not very many boys from Russian villages or small cities got as far as the tenth grade in the days when Chikatilo attended school. A high school education wasn't necessary to work on a collective farm or in a local factory. But for those who did make it, the logical step was to get out of "the sticks" and move to the cities where the universities are.

Andrei Chikatilo immediately left for Moscow, where he applied to the department of law at Moscow State University—a privileged faculty in the most prestigious university in the entire Soviet Union.

The Sumskoy Pedagogical Institute would have been much more accessible, but Chikatilo, who aspired to become leader of the Soviet Communist Party, would not consider a second-rate school.

Chikatilo claims that he passed all the pre-admission examinations for Moscow State University with the equivalent of A's and B's, but was ultimately turned down because—or so he says—of his repressed father. That is, he was rejected on political grounds.

Such an explanation is completely plausible. There are many instances of this actually happening. In ninety-nine cases out of one hundred, any stain on a person's political background was reason enough for rejection. Chikatilo thought he could be the lucky one and beat the system, but it did not work.

For the sake of argument, though, what if he had been accepted? The good student from the country, devoted to the communist ideal, would have had all the chances for a promising career. After all, he would have been the recipient of a higher degree in law, a native son of Russia's rural lands, and a family man. He might not have made a bad leader, either— certainly no worse than any of the others. To Chikatilo, it must have seemed that this rejection put an end to his childhood dream.

He returned home and enrolled in a local technical school for communications. A professional school did not necessarily close the door to one's ambitions, though it did make them more difficult to attain. Actually, it was considered a feather in one's cap to begin a career in the Party with a blue-collar background. But this path was closed to him as well. Steadfast in his political convictions and dogged in his studies, Chikatilo was deflected from his goals repeatedly by temptations of the flesh.

In 1955, a girl who was a friend of Andrei's sister developed a crush on him. He was tall, dark, nice-looking, and well read. Even though things hadn't worked out for him in Moscow, he still had a promising future ahead of him.

Andrei and his sister's friend began seeing each other. For a year and a half they were inseparable. He was kind and gentle, but when they finally decided to "go all the way," Andrei could not perform. For him, this failure was much more crushing than not getting into the university.

They tried a second time, in a meadow, with no one around for miles. Again, nothing happened. The same was true of a third attempt.

After the third time, they broke up. One can only imagine how the unsuccessful lover must have felt. The failure reminded him of the youthful vow he had broken, and again caused him to doubt his manhood. He must have viewed the opposite sex as being more and more out of reach.

For the time being, he postponed idea of sharing his life with a woman. After graduating from the communications school with excellent grades, he could have had his choice of jobs in his profession. Instead, he chose a more arduous path by heading eastward to the Urals to work on one of the country's monumental construction projects.

There, in the Siberian taiga 800 miles to the east of Moscow, he hauled cable and shimmied up poles. Summers were brutally hot and bug-infested; winters were numbingly cold. A person's fingers would stick to metal, and at night water would freeze in buckets. Having been raised in southern Russia, the drastic change in climate was a real shock to his system. But the main thing, according to a popular song on the radio to buck up everyone's spirits in these harsh conditions, was "to remain young at heart."

Such a project looked good on any résumé. At the same time, Chikatilo never abandoned his dream of continuing his studies. He began taking correspondence courses with the Moscow Electromechanical Institute. This lasted for two years, until he was called up for his obligatory military service. His plans of getting a degree in engineering had to be put on hold.

As far as his personal life at the time was concerned, Chikatilo tried, on a number of occasions, to find personal happiness with some of the local girls, but, again, his flesh was weak. While his peers enjoyed normal sexual relations, Chikatilo spent more time on his own, masturbating.

There were no sexual pathologists in the USSR in the 1950s to treat impotence. If there were, they were illegal. On the other hand, the country had always had its fair share of specialists in tropical medicine— as if palm trees, hummingbirds and tsetse-flies were in natural abundance.

In the summer of 1957, Andrei decided to take some time off from his construction project. He headed for Moscow to take part in the International Youth Festival. It was his first break after months of seven-day workweeks; for the country it was the first

real celebration since the Stalinist terror. People
danced and sang in the streets, alongside foreigners.
Naturally, the KGB kept an eye on any Soviet citizen
attempting to befriend them, but generally did not
interfere.

During the festival he met a nice young boy from
Europe, a fellow believer in communism. They corre-
sponded back and forth for as long as such things
were allowed. But a year later he was inducted into
the army, where he was exposed to sensitive military
material. As a result, he had to break off all contact
with foreigners. Even corresponding with relatives
abroad was strictly prohibited.

His first posting was with the border troops in
Central Asia. Afterward, he was assigned to special
communication troops in Berlin, the capital of the
German Democratic Republic, and the outpost of
socialism in Europe. Their task was to make sure the
top secret KGB lines from Berlin to Moscow were
functioning smoothly. It was also during this time he
became a member of the communist party. He would
remain one for almost twenty-five years, right up to
his expulsion in 1984—but more on that later.

Military service seemed to suit Andrei just fine.
He was working in his field of specialization, and not
in some hole, but in a European capital. To be sure,
the regime was strict, and there were no women
around to take a fellow's mind off his tasks. The
company of males also had its drawbacks—profanity,
taunts, obscene talk and gestures. With his supposed

puritanical streak, Andrei must have found that unbearable.

After Andrei had been demobilized from the army, he returned briefly to his native village. He lived at home with his parents and worked awhile on the collective farm, but city life was calling him back. He looked for a job in communications in Novocherkassk. One year later, in 1962, he moved to the neighboring region and the settlement of Rodionovo-Nesvetaiskaia, about twenty-five miles from Rostov. What caused this change of address is difficult to say. Even though Rodionovka, as it is called for short, is a regional center, it is still much smaller and more provincial than Novocherkassk. Maybe he was looking for work in more peaceful surroundings, or maybe a certain incident—which might have seemed perfectly innocent had it happened to someone other than Andrei Chikatilo—played a role.

The all-male brigade in which he worked was stretching cable from Rodionovka to the nearby village of Khotunok. After lunch one day, the group was taking a breather in the shade, talking idly and exchanging a few dirty jokes. Inevitably the conversation turned to their favorite topic—women. Because of his past experience with the opposite sex, Andrei always felt uncomfortable in the presence of such talk. He would blush or turn pale, provoking the harmless jeers of his comrades. On this particular occasion, the words he overheard must have conjured up such a suggestive image in his mind that he abruptly rose and hid among some trees further away.

A minute later the brigade leader went after him. Upon seeing what Andrei was doing in the privacy of the bushes, he lacked the sense to keep his mouth shut. When he returned, he loudly exclaimed to everyone what he had just witnessed. They all broke up laughing. Andrei was completely humiliated. For days to come, his coworkers made jokes at his expense, although never outside their immediate circle. It is quite possible that this incident caused him to lose his job with the brigade.

Life was relaxed and easy in Rodionovka. He rented a small apartment, beginning his string of success in finding places to live. He brought his parents from Yablochnoye to live with him, and eventually he bought them a hut of their own. His sister Tatyana got married there, where she lives to this day.

To supplement his earnings as a communications engineer, Chikatilo became a freelance reporter for a local newspaper. He contributed numerous articles and sketches to the paper for nearly a decade. He covered sporting events, or human interest stories about the achievements and contributions of his fellow villagers toward building a bright and happy future in "the first socialist country in the world." He enjoyed his job, and for obvious reasons. First of all, he was serving an important function, for Lenin himself had said that a newspaper was the best means of spreading the communist message to a mass audience. Second, anyone who worked for a newspaper had the respect and admiration of others. And, third, he loved having his own by-line.

His first small article was about a female colleague at work who had instantly caught his eye. Inexperienced in dealing with women, he decided to seduce her by writing about her accomplishments on the job. It worked. At one time, their co-workers even thought they would get married, but nothing came of it: Andrei was so bashful that he never got up the nerve to speak to her about anything personal.

Soon after, he began another romance. He wanted to get acquainted with a girl who worked in the library, where he often spent time. The problem was he didn't know how to go about doing it. Their conversation was limited to discussing books. By the time Andrei finally dared to make her a formal proposal, the librarian had already lost all interest in him.

However, the next attempt to fix up his personal life ended in triumph. His sister had a friend in Novoshakhtinsk, three years younger than Andrei. She was modest and hardworking—good housewife material. Tatyana brought them together and did everything in her power to make sure they married. Her efforts paid off. In 1963 Chikatilo wed Feodosya Semyonovna Odnacheva, "Fenya" for short.

They lived together for twenty-seven years, right up until the day of his arrest. Chikatilo never tired of repeating to anyone who would listen his undying love and devotion toward his wife. After everything that he had done to the other women, he always returned to his wife.

Feodosya Semyovna has since changed her last name, and moved to an undisclosed address. The following was taken from her testimony:

"We never had any intimate relations before we were married. From our very first night together, I sensed that he was sexually impotent. He could not consummate the sexual act without my help. At the time, I attributed it to shyness or modesty on his part."

One can feel sympathy for the young couple. They had no idea what to do. There was nowhere they could turn for consultation, and it was absolutely out of the question to see the usual doctors about their problem. Instead, they got along the best they could, maintaining the facade of a happy and well-adjusted couple.

The rare moments of success in their conjugal bed resulted in the birth of their daughter, Lyuda, in 1955, followed by a son, Yura, four years later.

Shortly before the birth of his daughter, Andrei had begun taking correspondence courses in Russian language and literature at Rostov University. He was then thirty years old. Because of family obligations, he studied in the evenings, after work. He simply had no time or energy left to spend on his colleagues at work or with his neighbors. As a result, he earned the reputation of an introvert. Even if he had had the extra time, it is unlikely he would have spent it with them, anyway. Compared to them, he was well read and aspiring to higher education—a specialist with a university education, and a second career as a freelance newspaper reporter.

The closer he came to getting his diploma, the more bored he became with his job in communications. It was not prestigious enough for a person of his ambitions. For the first and last time in his life, he got a job that can only be obtained with local communist party approval. It wasn't exactly an important position, but it carried a fancy title: chairman of the regional committee for physical education and sports.

Even from this low vantage point in the administrative and party hierarchy, his career still could have risen upward, though not as high as he had originally envisioned in his youthful daydreams. He had taken up his new, titled position rather late in life—he was thirty-four years old—but there was still a chance he could attain a highly respectable post further down the road. Many careers in the party had begun from similarly insignificant provincial posts.

A personal car and driver was not one of the "perks" offered to the regional chairman of physical education and sports, but he was given a motorcycle to visit the stadiums and gymnasiums in his region. His job mostly consisted of speaking to the champions of intramural competitions or junior athletic events. He was happily immersed in the world of adolescents, with whom he felt comfortable.

The adolescents also attracted his attention.

CHAPTER 10

Harmless Pranks

1970-1978

HAPPY AS HE WAS initially with his career in physical education, Chikatilo gradually grew restless. In 1970, he quit his job to devote himself to teaching Russian language and literature. For someone with a university education, it was a perfectly natural career move.

But Chikatilo had an ulterior motive for changing his profession. While watching young athletes at sporting events, he gradually came to the realization that he was aroused by the sight of half-clad young bodies. The odor of sweat in the locker rooms excited him, as did the young girls with barely visible breasts budding under their jerseys or the long-legged, narrow-hipped boys. He hated the idea that sooner or later the competitions would end and he would have to return to his office. He wanted to follow his charges into their dormitories and schools.

It did not take long for him to make his move.

Novoshakhtinsk Boarding School No. 32 needed a teacher of his background. Andrei Chikatilo was

161

readily hired, even though he had no previous experience.

What a thrill it must have been for him to walk up and down the aisles of his class, innocently placing his hand on a young girl's shoulder and then removing it in such a way that it would lightly graze her breast, even as he droned on about the classics of Russian literature to a bored audience. How wonderful it must have been, while explaining the finer points of Russian grammar, to scan the class from his teacher's desk in search of parted legs beneath short school dresses.

The only problem was that all the literary images and rules of grammar immediately slipped his mind once he began looking and touching. "What was it I was talking about?", he used to ask his students, trying to shake off his daydreams and immerse himself in their lessons. According to his colleagues, Chikatilo was rather listless and detached. His students didn't take him seriously, either—they smoked right in front of him in the classroom. He could stand silently, near the blackboard, for almost an entire class session, rocking slightly to and fro with his hands clasped behind his back.

The children noticed a certain absentmindedness about the new teacher, as did his colleagues though no one paid it much attention at first. Had it not been for his absentmindedness, he would have been given the job of principal when it became available. But he either forgot or confused just about everything. He even forgot about attending the mandatory meetings in the regional department of education, an oversight not easily forgiven. But in truth he did not want the job, as it would have taken him out of the classroom and away from his beloved children.

He lacked all sense of shame. Pulling up a chair next to a girl's desk, ostensibly to help with her homework, he would blatantly put his hand on her breast or knees. He had the habit of suddenly appearing in their sleeping quarters at night as the girls were getting undressed for bed. The girls would howl and scream, but he would just stand there silently, his eyes gleaming from behind his thick glasses as he stared at their half-naked bodies.

* * *

The girls were well aware of their teacher's "idiosyncracies." They were no secret to the other teachers either. Many of them noticed how Chikatilo would wander around the boarding school, his hands deep in his pockets, obviously fondling himself.

But none of this resulted in his firing, nor was he even limited in his direct access to the children. Two scandals were needed before his behavior was finally questioned.

On a warm day in May 1973, Chikatilo took his students to a nearby reservoir to go swimming. The children quickly undressed and dived into the water, shrieking and squealing. Some stayed close to shore; others swam out a bit further. As the water was not very deep, the teacher was not overly concerned. He also changed into his bathing suit and sat near the water's edge, observing his students. His gaze was most often drawn to fourteen-year-old Lyuba Kostina, the most developed girl in the class.

Lyuba was standing up to her ankles in the water and pulling on her rubber bathing cap. The water seemed cold to her, and she was debating whether to dive in. Her bathing suit, bought the year before, was now noticeably too small on her. Chikatilo had an overwhelming urge to run his hands over her pink loins.

He was close to thirty-seven years old.

"Come over here," he said softly to Lyuba. "I want to tell you something."

"Go away, Andrei Romanovich!"

Outside the classroom walls, students are allowed to address their teachers less formally.

Lyuba finally made up her mind, and splashed into the water. She dog-paddled slowly away from shore.

"I'm going to catch you now!" he said playfully, more for the benefit of the other students who might have overheard their conversation.

Though he wanted to control himself, he knew it was futile. His need was greater than any sense of shame.

He took a running leap into the water. With long, overhand strokes, he quickly caught up to the girl and grabbed her waist, made slippery by the water. Lyuba tried to break away, her arms and legs flailing, but still in a spirit of play. She was not afraid that anything bad might happen to her.

"Let me go," she cried. "Let me go, or else I'll drown!" Chikatilo didn't even think of letting her go.

He grabbed her breasts with both hands underwater and began gently fondling them. At first, Lyuba was not very alarmed. Boys had already made passes at her and she had always turned them down. But gradually the teacher began grabbing her so roughly that her breath caught. Now she realized this was serious.

She tried to break his grip, and begged him to let her go. She swallowed a mouthful of water and began coughing. He mumbled something incomprehensible. Holding her tightly with his left hand, he used his right hand to squeeze her hips and buttocks. Then all at once his hand disappeared under her suit.

The girl suddenly felt a sharp pain. The fingers of his large, rough hand were no longer touching her body but pinching and tearing. She began screaming. Her cries were heard from shore.

Instead of setting her free, Andrei asked her to scream even louder. Suddenly his body straightened up in the water, as if he were having a spasm, and he let her go.

Her friends led the sobbing girl out of the shallow water. She lay on the warm grass, moaning in pain.

He emerged from the water about ten minutes later. Without looking at anyone, he dressed quickly and disappeared.

All of Lyuba's classmates had seen what happened. Their parents found out about it that same day. The girl had suffered physical injury. Nevertheless, many people had closed their eyes in the past to the teacher's quirks and, as incredible as it sounds, they did so again.

But that was the last time Chikatilo would get off the hook so easily. A few days later, at the end of May, Chikatilo made one of his students, Tanya Gultseva, stay after class because of her poor command of Russian language and literature. It is difficult to say whether he really had intended to tutor her, or if he had planned beforehand to satisfy his lust.

With the girl seated behind her desk, Chikatilo asked her to open her textbook while he, in the meantime, strode over to the door and locked it.

What happened next is known from a statement the girl made: "He sat next to me at my desk and begin hugging and kissing me. His hands reached for my breasts, and he tried to take my panties off. I was frightened, and pushed him away. He scratched my legs and thighs. . . He went to unlock the door, and I took advantage of this by jumping out a window."

Soon after the January, 1979 murder of Lenochka Zakotnova, Andrei Chikatilo was taken in for questioning. He lied about the school incident to the police, saying he had locked Tanya Gultseva in the classroom so she would not be distracted from her studies. He said he had gone to the staff lounge to get something, and when he returned, the girl was gone.

When he was arrested and released in September 1984, he begrudgingly confessed, "I had an unfortunate incident in the boarding school. I committed impermissible actions with a student."

At the most recent inquest into the case, conducted in 1991, he talked about the same incident somewhat differently and in greater detail: "While helping her with her lessons, I noticed that her skirt had shifted up on her legs, exposing her panties and bare legs. This aroused me. I had a passionate desire to touch her breasts, legs, hips, genitals. She resisted, pushing me away and screaming. When she began screaming, I left her alone. When the director of the boarding school found out about it, I was forced to leave the school. As far as my attitude to Gultseva was concerned, I had no other intention than to commit perverse acts with her and to satisfy myself sexually as a result."

This last confession dates to the period when Chikatilo was already behind the bars of his isolation cell, when he had already confessed to everything else and when he had lost even the slightest hope of being released. He knew this harmless prank from eighteen years ago could add little to his guilt.

If he had understood at the beginning of his assaults that there is a certain line that people do not cross in everyday human relations, and more importantly, that the consequences for doing so could have led to his expulsion from the communist party, it is unlikely that he would have dared to do what he did later.

Back then in Novoshakhtinsk, there was no cause for "stricter" measures. He had faced some unpleasantries at work, and as a result he lost his job—but that was all. A paragraph in the criminal code provides rather strict punishment for acts of perversion committed with minors, yet it was not cited in an effort to nip his criminal activity in the bud.

The reasoning may have been that it was not worth it. It was considered an internal matter. Overall, Chikatilo was viewed as a good worker and a good communist. Moreover, he was a freelance reporter for a local newspaper and, besides, the organs of state security stood firmly behind one of their own.

The party itself tended to turn a blind eye to many personal foibles, demanding only that a person be "morally stable." In this case, Chikatilo was not censured at all.

He "voluntarily retired" and left the school quietly. Immediately thereafter, he found a new job at Technical School No. 39 in Novoshakhtinsk. This time, his pupils would be boys, but in the long run it made no difference. The main thing was that he was back among children and adolescents again.

*　*　*

Novoshakhtinsk is not a large city. Any news, especially of a scandalous nature, travels quickly, no matter how much one tries to suppress it. Feodosya Semyonovna soon found out about her husband's activities. Knowing him better than anyone else, she was absolutely shocked. She did not believe it.

She reasoned, because of their own miserable sex life at home, that he was just getting rid of pent-up energy Even though she wore the pants in the family, he was still a good provider. They had everything they needed. He loved their children, even spoiled them. If anything, he was a bit tight-fisted, but then he did not drink or smoke like other men who squandered their paychecks at the first opportunity they got. Thanks to his thriftiness, they were able to put aside a little each month for a new car they were hoping to buy.

As far as their relations in the bedroom were concerned, nothing had changed. As luck would have it, on one of the very few occasions when Chikatilo was able to complete the sex act, Feodosya became pregnant. Secretly, she had an abortion, hoping he would not find out—he had wanted more children.

Once by mistake, she mentioned the abortion and he had a fit. Afterwards, he cried tears of pity. But not for his wife. "They've torn my little child to pieces," he told her. "The doctors have killed my child."

He loved children—in his own way.

Sometimes this love manifested itself in unusual ways. One autumn day in 1983, he called to his wife's six-year-old niece, Marina, who was playing in their yard, to break away from her game and come see him. He was always so kind to her. As he stroked and patted her, he suddenly stuck his hand under her panties. Just then, someone came out onto the porch.

Reluctantly, he let the girl go. But he did not forget her.

On another occasion, Marina spent the night at her aunt's house. She slept in the same bed as Lyuda and Yura. In the middle of the night she was awakened by a ray of light falling on the face of her uncle, who was standing, completely naked, in the doorway. He whispered something to her, but the girl did not comprehend. Instead, she began to wake the other children. He left swiftly and silently, locking the door after him.

Later, when Marina had grown up, he again tried to get her alone. He took her for rides to the woods in his car, offered her money, and openly propositioned her.

* * *

The vocational school where Chikatilo taught was all male. By then, he was excited by boys as well as girls.

According to his colleagues, Chikatilo became even more withdrawn and aloof. Still, he performed his job competently. He even took his class on an excursion that passed without incident. In what can only be called outrageous irony, he continued to write newspaper articles about bringing up children in a spirit of morality and patriotism. He also became a freelance employee for another organization—the department of internal affairs, that is, the police, for whom he became an informer.

And last, but certainly not least, he finally achieved success with a woman during this period of his life. Chikatilo took a mistress.

Her name was Valentina Zh., the former wife of his own brother-in-law. For the first time in his life, he could be like other people sexually. He was euphoric.

He held the keys to an empty room in the school's dormitory. The woman was divorced from her husband, who was in prison. And Chikatilo's wife had long since given up questioning his whereabouts. He could always say that he was working late to meet a deadline for his paper, or that he was taking his students on an overnight field trip. Even more believable, he could say that he was on assignment in his new freelance position, the nature of which had to be kept secret.

This was to be his only normal relationship with a woman.

Investigator Yandiev, when he learned of the affair, began searching for the woman in 1991. He brought her before Chikatilo for a face to face meeting, hoping to force some reaction that would help explain or give insight into the killer.

The woman looked at her former lover, now accused of the most heinous crimes, with unconcealed horror. Chikatilo, for his part, could not stop grinning from the memories of those days spent with her fifteen years earlier.

The motives for his frequent changes of address remain a mystery to us—and perhaps to the investigators, too. In all likelihood, he was let go from the technical school due to a reduction in staff. Another possibility is that a superior ordered that he be fired. Whatever the reason, in September 1978 he moved his family from their apartment in Novoshakhtinksk to the dormitory of a local vocational school in Rostov. Both he and his wife found work at this school—he as an instructor and she as a superintendent.

During the night, as Chikatilo's former pupils recall, their new instructor liked to look in on them as they were sleeping. Ever so quietly, so as not to wake his wife and children, he stole along the corridors on tiptoe, opening the doors to their rooms.

Volodya Shcherbakov, ten years old at the time, has vivid memories of Chikatilo's nocturnal wanderings. One evening, after visiting his parents, he returned to the dormitory with some homemade sweets. Fearing that the older students would steal them, he asked the instructor to let him sleep in one of the empty rooms. The man obliged by putting Volodya in the room next to his.

In the middle of the night, the boy felt something strange. A hot and sweaty face was pressed against his stomach. He opened his eyes and saw the instructor bending over him. The boy became alarmed and jumped out of bed. Chikatilo immediately vanished. In the morning, he acted as if nothing had happened. The boy wisely held his tongue.

A similar incident occurred just a few nights later. This time, Volodya threatened to scream and wake

everyone up. Only then did Chikatilo leave him
alone. By then, the new instructor's unusual habits
were no secret to the other students or to his colleagues.

Chikatilo roamed the corridors of the school with
a vacant expression on his face, oblivious to everything around him. He did not even attempt to discipline his increasingly unruly students who laughed
at him and called him "Goose" because of his long
neck and prominent adam's apple. From time to
time, the director of the school, Andreyev, had to call
him into his office for a lecture, but it was like
talking to a brick wall. When the director later recognized his teacher from the police sketch, he was not
the least bit surprised—Chikatilo was capable of anything.

In the fall of 1985, excited by the proximity of the
children he longed for, yet frustrated by their inacces-
sibility, Chikatilo began scouring the city of Shakhty
from one end to the other. Soon the city would not be
enough for him. His search for fresh victims would
take him out into the region and around the country.
He began hanging around school bathrooms. Though
he was not a particularly generous person by nature,
he started handing out gum to young children in the
hope that sooner or later one would follow him to a
secluded area.

It is quite possible that while he was teaching at
the vocational school, Chikatilo was not even sure
himself how to satisfy his lust. He knew that cries
for help excited him, but he had yet to smell the

scent of blood. He liked to inflict pain on others, but not so far as to cause someone's death.

On December 22, 1978, he finally understood what he needed. On that day he raped and killed Lenochka Zakotnova.

On that day his life changed drastically.

CHAPTER 11

The Trail of Blood

1979-1984

AT THE END OF 1978, Andrei Chikatilo's life of
crime turned from pink to bright red.

He dropped out of sight for awhile. It is known
that he continued to work in the same vocational
school, maintained the same address in Shakhty, and
kept his one-room shack on Mezhevoy Lane.

He was obviously afraid. Conducting himself like
a churchmouse, he even performed his job more or
less satisfactorily, which was not like him at all.
Clearly he understood that at any moment, he could
be called in by the police for questioning.

Then rumors began to spread around the city that
the girl's killer had been arrested. An ex-convict
named Kravchenko from Mezhevoy Lane was the
culprit.

Chikatilo could breathe a sigh of relief. Unable to
control himself any longer, he took up the old habits
characteristic of his "pink" period.

One day, three six-year-old girls—Lena, Ksyusha
and Irina—walked into the instructor's room, where
he was sitting by himself. They needed some old

newspapers for a little bonfire they wanted to make out in the courtyard.

Any responsible adult might have tried to talk the children out of such a dangerous activity. But Chikatilo could not refuse the young girls, as he could not refuse children in general. He took each in turn by the hand, pretending to look for the newspapers, all the while molesting them.

He later described the incident in his customary style. "It was during the summer. They were all wearing short dresses, which provoked my interest. I slapped their fannies and stuck my hand under their panties."

The "interest" he had taken in the three girls became known that evening to their parents, but, once again, inexplicably, they took no action against him. If they had wanted to, they could have easily had him arrested, but either ignorance or intimidation held them back.

As far as we know, this is the last episode of his "pink" period. After this, he stopped bothering children. That is, they no longer would live to tell about it.

He now had an entirely different modus operandi.

He had already killed once. Two and a half years would pass before he killed again. Then the killings would come more frequently, but there would be an explanation for the pauses in between. Why was the first interval so long?

One can assume that he feared being arrested. But after Kravchenko was put in jail, the fear gradually dissipated. He had found something else to comfort him—another woman.

By an incredible coincidence, the woman was the older sister of Irina Dunenkova, the retarded girl whom he would eventually rape and kill two years later in Aviators' Park.

They met for the first time in the spring of 1981 on a suburban commuter train. The girl, along with one of her friends, rented Chikatilo's shack at 26 Mezhevoy Lane. This wretched abode, however, was not the site of their trysts. Perhaps the presence of the other girl inhibited him, or maybe he felt more confident outdoors. In any case, their meetings took place in remote country areas.

The two would arrive at their prearranged meeting place together, although they would act as if they did not know one another. Chikatilo demanded that their relations be kept an absolute secret. He always had his briefcase with him, in which he carried a bottle of wine.

Once, when the girl was slightly tipsy, she tried to see what else was inside the briefcase. Extremely irritated, Chikatilo moved the case closer to himself. The contents of his briefcase at the time are unknown.

It was stated earlier that Valentina Zh. was Chikatilo's first and last lover. If that is the case, what was this other woman's relation to him?

Strictly speaking, Valentina was indeed the only woman with whom he enjoyed normal sexual relations. This was not the case with Dunenkova.

According to her testimony, Chikatilo, after he had drunk his customary single glass of wine, soon realized that his capabilities did not correspond to his desire. With his partner's consent, he resorted to various forms of manipulation, by which he was finally able to satisfy himself.

This more or less confirms the words of his wife, Feodosya: "From 1981-1982, my husband became more and more impotent. I'm a healthy woman, and I wanted to be intimate with him. During the last six to seven years, whenever I asked him to be with me, he would always refuse. He would say, 'Do you want a stallion for a husband?' We had practically no sexual intimacy."

Why did Chikatilo not kill Dunenkova, as he later killed the other women who voluntarily followed him into the woods?

Investigator Yandiev asked Chikatilo this same question. He replied that it was because she was a remarkable woman, tolerant of his weakness. She did not get angry like the others when he was unable to perform. Instead, she acquiesced to the "various forms of manipulation." He did not touch her. But the others, who had mocked him and wounded his male pride, had to pay for it.

This explanation seems perfectly logical. The weaker a person is, the greater his pride. However, we believe there is maybe another reason why Dunenkova did not suffer the same horrible fate as all the others. Chikatilo had thus far escaped punishment, but was not yet sure enough in his activities to know he would not be discovered. He needed time to become assured of his invincibility, of his superiority in relation to the law.

Like the profile of other recent serial killers, Andrei Chikatilo is a completely average person. He does not particularly stand out in any way. He became the "killer of the century" only because of the great number of victims. Another Russian, Mikhosevich, claimed 38 lives. The Colombian Pedro Alonso Lopez was indicted for 300 murders, but the remains of only fifty-three—a strange coincidence—were found. Chikatilo was *allowed* to become a serial killer, having been freed by the police at least twice. What is characteristic of all these killers, and serial murderers in general, is their feeling of exclusivity from others, a belief in their ability to mock the law at every turn.

After the death of Lena Zakotnova, and even after the police set him free and left him alone, Chikatilo still did not believe he was above the law. He was extremely cautious as he keenly followed the progress of Kravchenko's case, which was being played out in the courts. For the time being he had to keep his activities at bay until Kravchenko was sentenced.

Chikatilo may have been the only person who was genuinely glad to see Kravchenko shot. As long as Kravchenko was alive, and for as long as there existed the possibility that at any minute the case against him could be dropped, Chikatilo was obliged to keep a very low profile.

He changed his place of work—got away from his colleagues who knew too much about him; away from the minors who incited his lust; and away from his profession of teaching—that is, away from all forms of temptation. He had to bide his time patiently.

On September 3, 1981, Chikatilo committed his second murder. The victim was seventeen-year-old Larisa Tkachenko, a student at a vocational school. The site was the left bank of the Don—"Levberdon." It was the only time he killed without a knife. We can only speculate that he had been lying low for so long that he had for so long that he had neglected to resort to his usual methods.

* * *

In March 1981, Chikatilo made an unusual, but logical, career move. A failure as a teacher, he switched to industry, where he was hired as a supply clerk in the supplies department of a huge industrial complex called Rostovnerud. Feodosya Semyonovna also got a job there, as a forwarding agent.

In the planned Soviet economy, everything had been determined from the center. Moscow dictated how much of what to give to whom, right down to the last nail or piece of thread, regardless of any laws of supply and demand.

That was how the Soviet economy worked in theory. In practice, it made no difference how goods and services were distributed—there were rampant shortages of both everywhere. Yet, the system somehow continued to function in its rickety fashion. And the only ones who knew where to find the hidden supplies—literally the nuts and bolts of Soviet industry—were the more resourceful and persistent supply clerks. This system gave birth to a special class of people, popularly known as *tolkachi*, or "pushers," from the Russian verb to push.

In order to become a good supply clerk, one did not necessarily need to have a commanding knowledge of industry or be a specialist. It did not hurt, of course, but there was no particular advantage to it. Any person, regardless of background, could become a first-class supply clerk. Former circus jugglers, pharmacists, retired naval officers, unsuccessful film directors, and dancers, among others, have all held the position at one time or another.

A supply clerk must be ready to move at a moment's notice, to gather his belongings and rush off to the nearest factory, or cross the eleven time zones of the country from the Baltics to the Far East, and back again. He has to be able to find a common language with ticket sellers and porters, secretaries and general directors, drivers and telephone operators. He absolutely must know the ins and outs of giving, and taking, bribes under the table. He must be agile, sharp-witted, urbane, unpretentious and, perhaps, a bit thievish. That is the ideal portrait.

Supply clerk Andrei Chikatilo was no great find for Rostovnerud. In three years of working there, he was more like a weight around the company's neck.

His colleagues were grateful whenever they were rid of him. Still, no one had any personal complaints about him. He was generally pleasant, calm and polite. When they read in the papers about his alleged crimes, they were incredulous—it could not possibly be the same Andrei Romanovich.

For Chikatilo, the new job must have been a gold mine. First of all, he was granted access to all kinds of materials and tools that are normally impossible to buy. No one would notice if he were to take home a few boards, a sheet of metal, or a set of wrenches. In addition, any repairs on his car were taken care of. All he had to do was pull up to the nearest shop— who would refuse the supply clerk? Too much depended upon his decisions.

As an insight into his character, Chikatilo was scrupulously precise in the matter of personal expenses. He made sure he was reimbursed for every little expense associated with a business trip, including bus rides that cost mere pennies. Whenever he could, he added others' receipts to his own expense sheet.

Another benefit to this job was that the salary was more than he got at the vocational school, and bonuses were handed out from time to time. Still, that was not the main appeal. A job that would keep him on the road had its own advantages: today he would be in Rostov, tomorrow in Bataisk, the day after in Novocherkassk. He could buy food for his family in one place, a pair of slippers for his wife in another. This, too, was indisputably useful, but it

was still not the most important aspect of the job—
which was that it gave him freedom.

There would be no bosses or subordinates to
pester him. He would warn his family that he was
going on a business trip and that he would be back in
two days, or three—depending on how things worked
out. If he went somewhere accompanied by a driver,
he would invariably send him back alone, saying he
would handle the rest of the job on his own. No one
checked to see if he really needed that extra day, or if
he was just hanging around.

Chikatilo later justified his crimes by saying that
life on the road made him wild. Away from family
and friends, surrounded by drunks, he could not
relax, eat home-cooked meals, or sleep in his own
warm bed.

In reality, he wandered around train and bus stations and slept on benches, when in fact he was only
an hour's ride from home. He became intoxicated
with his newfound freedom.

And he envied those whom he despised.

"I had to spend a good deal of time in stations, on
trains, commuter trains, and buses. There are all
sorts of vagrants in these places. They beg, demand,
and steal, and get drunk first thing in the morning.
These vagrants lure minors. I had to witness scenes
of their sexual behavior in the stations and on the
commuter trains. It reminded me of my own failures
as a man. I asked myself, 'Do these low-lifes have the
right to exist?' It was no problem getting to know
them. They were very forward, asking for money,

food, vodka, and offering themselves for sex. I saw how they sneaked off with their partners to secluded places."

He gave this statement during an interrogation session on March 23, 1990, just a few days before he began confessing to everything, including crimes he was not even accused of. His envy had turned into hatred for everyone who was free. He had to convince himself, and others, that he was just as good as they were. Maybe he was guilty, but it was their fault, not his. If only these degenerate types did not exist in Soviet society. . .

It was only after he was arrested that Chikatilo tried to find a basis for his criminal actions. But in the early nineteen-eighties, he had roamed the railway stations and bus depots without rhyme or reason, totally consumed with lust.

Unfortunately for Larisa Tkachenko, Chikatilo often visited the central branch of the Rostov library on Engels Street to read his favorite communist newspapers. It was at the bus stop where Engels crosses Voroshilovsky Avenue that he spotted Tkachenko.

At the time, he did not have a specific plan. Later, when the killings mounted, sometimes with only a week in between, it was as if he were acting on automatic pilot. This time, he was improvising. The girl was young and carefree. It did not take a great deal of effort on his part to get her to follow him. She agreed to walk with him to the left bank of the Don. What he promised her is not known.

Chikatilo was not especially prepared for this walk in the woods. He did not even have a knife in his briefcase. Instead, he used his bare hands to strangle her. That was the last time he did it that way—there was no sexual thrill in it. Or, if there was, it was not as intense as when he saw blood.

From that moment onward he killed only with knives, although on some occasions he used a rock, if one happened to be lying nearby, to bludgeon his victims.

On that day he led the promiscuous seventeen-year-old Tkachenko to the forest path on Levberdon and undressed her without any resistance. Once again, his flesh betrayed him.

"It was clear that she would agree to anything. I should have loved this young girl and thanked her for bringing pleasure to an old man. But I obviously didn't require sexual pleasure from the caresses of a young girl. Someone else, some kind of beast, was living within me. I began to choke her. I stuffed earth into her mouth and hit her with my fists. After I ejaculated, I pushed my sperm into her vagina and rectum. I also shoved a stick into her vagina, and I bit off a nipple."

He never went hunting again without a knife. All his talk about not being able to restrain himself or being overcome by waves of lust was nothing but lies. After this murder, the rest were all premeditated.

The next time he killed, ten months later, he had a knife with him. Tired of waiting for his bus to come, he decided to walk to the village of Donskoy along the highway. Along the way he caught up with a thirteen-year-old girl who had also given up on the bus. He struck up a conversation with her. Her name was Lyuba.

They walked along together for about half a mile, before turning off into a wooded area path that stretched out along the highway. He stopped here. Certain that no one was around, he undressed and killed her. His weapon of choice was a folding knife with a blade that was sharpened on both sides. It was the first knife in his collection of twenty-three.

More than forty wounds were counted on Lyuba Biryuk's body, discovered a few days later.

"The flow of blood, coupled with the victim's agony, brought me pleasure, and I continued stabbing her."

Now he knew exactly how to overcome his impotence. He could care less at what price.

* * *

Chikatilo had been working in the supply department at Rostovnerud for more than a year. It was time for him to take his annual one-month vacation, beginning July 21, only nine days after the murder of Lyuba Biryuk. His wife packed him off to take in the hot baths of Goryachii Klyuch, literally "Hot Spring," a resort area outside the city of Krasnodar.

He returned home three weeks later, explaining rather incoherently to Feodosya Semyonovna that his

vacation had gone all wrong from the very beginning.
He had been unable to purchase the necessary
voucher that would have allowed him to get his
meals and hot water treatment at the spa. In general,
he had concluded, it was better to stay home than
waste time in resorts. He wriggled out of the question as to why he had not come home sooner, if
things were really that bad.

The reason he had not returned home right away
is that, on the fourth day of his vacation, he raped
and killed fourteen-year-old Lyuba Volobuyev in a
sorghum field near the Krasnodar Airport. The girl
had taken a flight earlier in the day from
Novokuznetsk and was waiting at the airport to
catch a connecting flight to visit relatives.

For almost three weeks Chikatilo had loitered in
the Krasnodar area, without making a single attempt
to go home. On August 13, he traveled outside the
city to go swimming in a pond. On the bus he
became acquainted with Oleg Pozhidayev, a nine year
old boy. They walked a short distance from the pond
and into a wooded area near the settlement of Enem.

That evening Oleg's parents reported him
missing, but long hours of searching turned up
nothing. Chikatilo's memory, usually excellent,
sometimes failed him. He was unable to remember
exactly the place in the woods where he had added
Pozhidayev to his growing body count. To this day
the boy's remains have not been found.

He had still not reported back to work after his
so-called vacation when he killed sixteen-year-old

Olga Kuprina. After watching her light up one cigarette after another as she stood on the platform between railway cars, he engaged her in conversation and found out that she had just had a big argument with her mother and now was taking a ride, with no particular destination, just to get her mind off the unpleasantness. He offered her money to go for a walk with him.

They got off at the first stop, Kazachii Lagerya, and headed in the direction of a shelterbelt adjacent to the railroad tracks. "The girl's cries," he said at the investigation, "and the way she moved while I was stabbing her with my knife drove me into a state of sexual frenzy."

After satisfying his bloodthirsty lust three times in three weeks, Andrei Chikatilo returned to his job. He was no more successful at fulfilling his job obligations than he was his duties as a husband. Everyone who worked with him at Rostovnerud had the same opinion of him: he didn't know the business, nor was he remotely interested in it. As one fellow employee put it, "his head was in the clouds." Everything that went on at the huge industrial conglomerate, where hundreds of people worked, held absolutely no meaning for him. He would do whatever he was told to do—if he remembered. During meetings in the director's office, he sat in silence, staring off into space or yawning.

He behaved in approximately the same manner at his trial in 1991. While mothers fainted from the endless litany of horrible crimes, witnesses testified

against him, the judge addressed him, and photojournalists snapped his picture, he yawned. He sat on his
bench, turned to the side, behind the iron rods of his
cage, and opened his mouth convulsively as if
gasping for air, or as if bored with the whole spectacle.

After the morning planning meetings in the
director's office, he returned to his department. He
was invariably polite and proper with his subordinates, but more often than not he found it difficult to
give them specific assignments. Even when he wrote
down instructions in his little notebook, he still
could not remember what he was supposed to do. His
coworkers all recall the times he would sit for hours
at a time at his desk, making entries in his notebook.
One time they looked and saw that he was drawing
little crosses. That was when they decided "he was
not all there."

Most of the time his thoughts were concentrated
on getting out of the office as soon as possible for a
short business trip—even for a few days—to Rostov,
Bataisk, Novocherkassk, Novoshakhtinsk, or Krasny
Sulin. It really didn't matter where, just as long as it
took him away from his director, who lectured him,
and his coworkers, who once, as a practical joke,
placed a brick in his briefcase. Only after he had carried it all the way home did he realize it was there.

The only times he showed any signs of life were
when he visited Tamara Aleksandrovna Zhukova, the
woman in charge of recording employees' business
trips, to obtain the necessary documents for his next

official leave. According to her, Chikatilo was extremely polite—all "please" and "thank you's." She understood that these trips were very important to him and could not be postponed. As soon as the papers were filled out, he was out the door. There were times when his coworkers, assuming he was away on a business trip, ran into him at the bus station or on a commuter train. On such occasions he would act as if he did not know them and make himself scarce at the first opportunity, walking the whole length of the train to get away. In general, he walked the trains from one end to the other, his eyes darting left and right for potential victims.

* * *

Chikatilo's first three murders were committed cautiously, ineptly and nervously, with long intervals in between.

The second three, carried out during his vacation, were handled with more finesse and resolve. Beginning with these murders, he made sure he always had a knife with him.

From then on, his "schedule" looked like this:

1982—June 12, July 25, August 13, second half of August, September (twice), December 11;

1983—June, July (three times), August 9, August-September, September-October, October 27, December 27;

1984—January 9, February 21, March 24, May 25, June 10, June-July, July 19, end of July, August 2,

August 7, August 8-15, second half of August, August 29, September 6.

Not all dates have been precisely established. He did not mark the dates in his notebook. When relatives announced a person missing, or when a corpse turned up shortly after a murder, there usually was no problem in establishing a date. Sometimes, though, the forensic specialists had great difficulty determining the precise moment death had occurred.

The regularity of his killing in the summers of 1982 and 1983 and all of 1984 are particularly striking. The breaks in rhythm in fall of 1982 and winter of 1983, as well as the two-month lull in spring of 1984, might be attributed to seasonal hazards for a "lone wolf" to be roaming about.

It is impossible to determine whether Chikatilo planned his hunts in advance. But what is apparent is that he was becoming more experienced in finding new ways to lure his victims to their deaths. By the end of 1983, he had established his own "signature." If he came upon a young girl of loose morals or a prostitute, he would offer her money or alcohol to go off with him to some secluded place. Sometimes all he would promise was the chance to have sex with him, a strong and well-built man at the height of his prowess. This was the preferred method, since it didn't involve any out-of-pocket expenses, even though it really made little difference in the long run; he always knew beforehand how these meetings would end.

Whenever Chikatilo encountered a respectable-looking young woman, he would usually offer to help her get wherever it was she needed to go. He especially preyed on those who were traveling from home to some place they had never been before. He had an excellent sense of direction, and he studied bus routes and train schedules. He was always ready to point out the shortest distance between two points, volunteering to take a person to wherever the buses ran more frequently or where it would be easier to flag down a passing vehicle. His appearance and soft-spoken manner won the trust of his victims-to-be.

His approach with children was different. For them, Chikatilo had concrete temptations in the form of gum and candy, or hypothetical gifts of stamps, videocassette, or delicious home-cooked meals, all at his imaginary dacha at the other end of a forest path. Chikatilo had taken courses in education at the university level, and he had worked with children for many years. Maybe he had failed as a teacher, but the years of experience told him what to promise to whom.

His method of killing also followed a specific pattern. Invariably he held the knife in his left hand and maintained a certain distance from his victim to avoid being splattered with blood. "I learned how to stay clean. I worked the knife with my left hand. I write with my right hand, but when I cut food I hold the knife in my left." After he was arrested, he demonstrated his method to investigators on man-

An unidentified corpse—another of Chikatilo's victims.

Relatives of the victims
outside the courthouse.

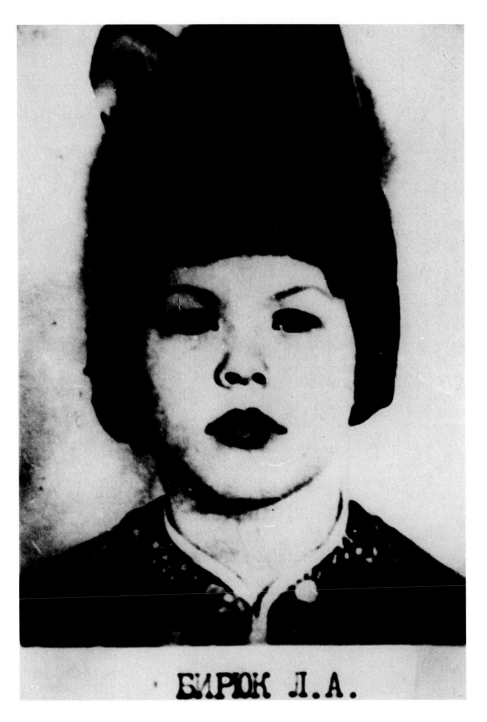

Lyuba Biryuk—one of the victims.

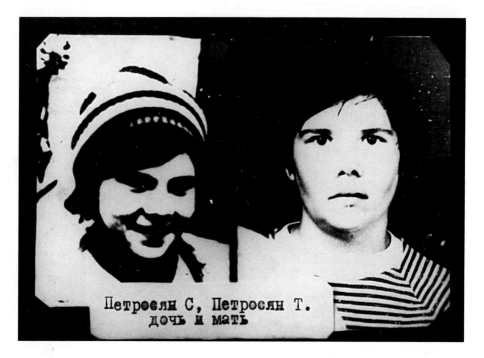

Svetlana and Tatyana Petrosyan—mother and daughter.
Chikatilo killed them in the forest shelter-belt near Shakhty.

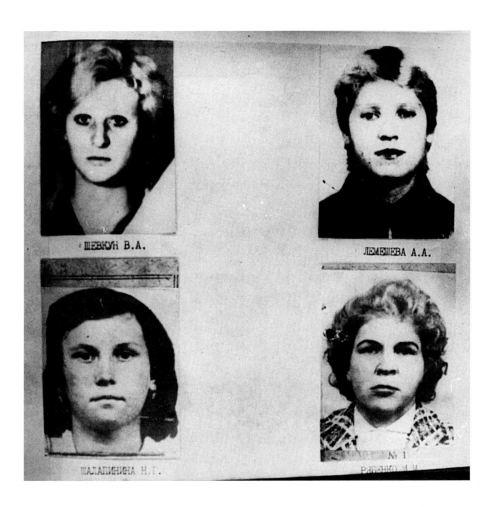

Some of Chikatilo's victims (clockwise from top left):
Vera Shevkun, Anna Lemesheva, Marta Ryabenko,
Natalya Shalapinina.

Using a mannequin, Chikatilo demonstrates how he killed his victims.

Bus station in Rostov-on-Don, where Chikatilo searched for and
eventually found many of his victims. He was arrested here by
Aleksandr Zanosovsky in 1984.

The outbuilding in Shakhty. Chikatilo owned this shanty
from 1978–1982. It was here that he killed his first victim—a
girl named Lena Zakotnova.

nequins. He truly did cut up the bodies as if cutting food, but he claimed he never ate human flesh.

Due to the absence of any survivors or witnesses of his attacks, it is impossible to verify the accuracy of this last statement, but it appears likely that cannibalism played a part in at least some of his murders. Some body parts, like tips of tongues or nipples, he would normally bite off with his teeth; others he would cut off using one of his twenty-three knives ("with the right hand I pulled out the uterus and with the left I sliced it").

At times he would throw away the parts; other times, he stuffed them inside wounds. He confirmed that on occasion he would take a piece of flesh in his mouth, but he insisted that he never swallowed. If that is so, it leaves unanswered why none of the cut or bitten pieces were ever found. Chikatilo said he did not remember what he had done with them.

During his interrogation, Chikatilo testified that from time to time he stuck a frying pan inside his briefcase. His explanation was that it was often impossible to predict beforehand what he might need on a business trip. It is chilling to contemplate what he may have cooked in the frying pan, when one considers that the remains of small campfires were discovered near a murder site on more than one occasion.

Primitive people believe that a person can acquire strength, intellect, courage and health from eating the flesh of an enemy. Although no evidence exists that supports the hypothesis, it cannot be ruled out that Chikatilo cooked and ate the organs of sexual reproduction and sexual pleasure in the hope that it would restore his potency and make him feel a complete man. He had admitted once he was constantly angered by the fact that young boys had no problem as far as that part of their body was concerned, while he, much taller and bigger, had nothing but trouble. This envy, which gradually turned into hatred, could have led to the cutting off and gnawing of his victims' genitals.

Another beastly aspect of his killing is not from the realm of hypothesis, but an established fact—the "partisan" ritual. He ran around the mutilated bodies, waving the bloody pieces of flesh and imagining himself to be a courageous partisan fighter from one of his favorite books. Gory as that was, undoubtedly the most cold-blooded and abominable feature of his murders is that as he became more skilled, he was able to cut his victims to allow the bloodletting he craved, but not their instant deaths. He had become a diabolical surgeon who knew how to prolong his victims' agony while he performed all manner of sexual perversion on them.

Experts found marks on the bodies of his victims that showed that the murderer, without removing his knife, would rain down dozens of blows in one place as if imitating the movements of intercourse. Sexual pathologists view this as a kind of ritual masturbation. Another feature of his signature was the unusual pattern of stab wounds made around the eyes.

Amazing too is that he did not attempt to cover his tracks. He did not bury, hide, or drag the corpses off to remote places. Instead, he covered them with earth, leaves, or old newspapers before quietly leaving the scene.

When he returned home from a business trip, he unpacked his suitcase and hid the knives in one place. "Hid" is not exactly the right word for it—he simply put them in one place. They were easily uncovered during the search of his apartment. One other peculiarity was that he had three suits—black, gray and brown—and in each he carried a different knife so he would not have to move them from one suit to another.

After a long and exhausting day carrying around his briefcase, and after a good meal—he always had a healthy appetite—he would go to bed, always sleeping on the same side and never changing position during the night. He fell asleep instantly and slept soundly without any dreams until morning. He dressed and went to work, where he dozed at the meetings and drew little crosses. The scolding and berating he suffered at the hands of his director increased with time. In the past he had reacted indifferently to such treatment, but now he became more indignant and offended, complaining outright to his coworkers about the injustice and slights he had to put up with daily. No one had ever recalled him doing that before.

The director's patience with his supply chief was wearing thin, and complaints about him were being voiced with greater frequency. Chikatilo was growing more and more resentful, although he continued to be outwardly calm and polite, if somewhat withdrawn, with his coworkers.

Normally not given much to talking, Chikatilo could suddenly become very sociable, especially after a glass of vodka. He became downright garrulous whenever conversation switched to the topic of how no one appreciated him at work. Whenever he retreated into his shell during the investigation, the only way for investigators to get a reaction from him was to ask about his relationship with the managers at Rostovnerud. This would immediately unleash a torrent of harsh words about the scoundrels who terrorized him. Once he had gathered momentum, he would answer one question after another, and often in great detail.

He would attribute the murders that followed in rapid succession in 1983-84 to the special requirements of his job, the chaos at work and imagined persecutions from his superiors. All these business trips were "insane," and had made him "wild," resulting in his descending to the level of the degenerates who spent their time hanging around train stations and sleeping on commuter trains. He claimed his reputation was "poisoned" at work.

He ended up in train stations and on commuter trains not because he was forced into taking "insane" business trips, but because he consciously chose to be there. And his name had not been "poisoned"—in fact, he was made an offer to leave of his own accord without interruption in his salary and other privileges that accrue to a Soviet worker who has put in many years at one job. That was one of the inexplicable paradoxes of the Soviet system—the law protected loafers, drunks, and incompetents from losing their jobs as long as they showed up at work and did not break any rules. Upon being fired, the indignant worker could always turn to the courts for protection, and the courts would always get him reinstated.

Although he slept through meetings, forgot important details and in general slacked off on the job, it was practically impossible for the director of Rostovnerud to remove his detested supply clerk. Had it not been for the theft of a car battery, there would have been virtually no way to get rid of Chikatilo and others like him.

He was accused of stealing a battery and a roll of linoleum in 1984, when he already had more than twenty deaths on his conscience. The consequences for stealing state property were harsh under Soviet law—sometimes invoking the death sentence—but at the same time, theft was an integral part of daily life. The charge for stealing linoleum was later dropped for lack of evidence, but the incident with the battery cost him his membership in the communist party and a short jail sentence.

It is entirely plausible he did steal them. After all, both items were chronically in short supply, and every kitchen needs linoleum; every car a battery. As far as the roll of linoleum was concerned, Chikatilo insisted that his driver had not delivered it to the warehouse but, instead, sold it to someone along the way. But, as head of the supplies department, he would be stuck with the blame.

In any event, his relations with the managers at Rostovnerud were irreparably soured from that point on. The director saw that it was the right time to make a move. A person of his stature in a small city is an important figure, one whose opinions are listened to and respected. Criminal charges were filed against Chikatilo. Public prosecutor Valery Tarshin was put in charge of the case.

He called Chikatilo in for questioning. The suspect tried to persuade the prosecutor that he was an educated man with intellectual needs, and that it would be absolutely absurd to think that he would risk both his job and party career over such nonsense. But no matter how elegantly he tried to finesse the situation, his words had no effect on Tarshin.

Chikatilo panicked. He began contradicting himself, and mixing up his responses to Tarshin's questions. In the middle of the investigation, he unexpectedly fled to Rostov, on the pretext that his vacation was due. This raised some eyebrows. Innocent people, as a rule, do not suddenly run away from an investigation, especially if they are trying to clear their name.

Tarshin issued a subpoena for his return, but Feodosya Semyonovna assured the prosecuter that her husband had left for some well-deserved rest. Meanwhile, Chikatilo was holed up in Rostov, looking for a new job.

In the early days of August, he was hired to head the supply division at a Rostov industrial complex called Spetsenergoavtomatika. When his former bosses in Shakhty found out, they breathed a collective sigh of relief and dropped all charges against him. Tarshin, figuring that the matter did not warrant any further attention, stopped sending his subpoenas. It probably would have been completely forgotten, were it not for Chikatilo's arrest the following month.

In the meantime, Chikatilo must have been breathing a sigh of relief himself. The nightmare in Shakhty was behind him, and his new job held the possibility of even greater mobility. Virtually free to go wherever he pleased, he could take longer and more serious business trips, in addition to the usual short junkets around the region. New horizons had opened before him.

On August 8, 1984, barely settled into his new job, he flew to Tashkent, the capital of the Central Asian republic of Uzbekistan. He left behind two bodies after a week-long stay.

On the outskirts of Tashkent, near the river Chirchik where he had gone for a swim, he met a young, inebriated woman whose name was never established. He killed her in his usual fashion, but for good measure he cut off her head and threw it in the bushes.

A few days later he was in a commuter train heading out to the countryside to buy melons. Ever the dutiful family man, Chikatilo always brought something home from his business trips. He caught sight of ten-year-old Akmaral Saidaliev. They detrained at the first stop. He stabbed her with a kitchen knife and bludgeoned her in a cornfield.

On August 2, before his trip, Chikatilo had murdered Natalya Golosovskaya. Five days later, with his airplane ticket to Tashkent already in his pocket, he met seventeen-year-old Lyudmila Alekseyeva in Rostov and "showed her the way" to the left bank of the Don. In the woods near a hotel, he slashed the girl thirty-nine times with a kitchen knife. He also cut off her upper lip and stuffed it in her mouth, hacked up her breasts and disemboweled her. From the victim he took ninety rubles, a cosmetics case and a few other minor items.

After the murder of Alekseyeva, which happened late in the evening, Chikatilo did not return home. Instead, he spent the night in the office at his new job. A coworker, I.A. Kovalev, found him when he arrived at work in the morning, washing his shirt in the bathroom sink.

In that same "poisoned" state of mind, and after having returned from Uzbekistan, he killed eleven-year-old Sasha Chepel on August 28. It was also after work, in the same place he had snuffed out Alekseyeva's life, and with the same knife. Again, he returned to the office and spent the night sleeping at his desk. Although his coworker must have thought it odd, he kept his thoughts to himself—what business was it of his if his colleague had worked himself too hard during the day and stayed all night?

On September 6, he killed twenty-four-year old Irina Luchinskaya in Aviators' Park with the same knife—evidently, he must have been wearing the same suit. For the third straight time, he slept at his desk.

Exactly one week later, he was arrested by Captain Aleksandr Zanosovsky and his partner after they had followed him for many hours. In Chikatilo's briefcase they found a dirty towel, a skein of strong rope, a jar of vaseline, a kitchen knife with a plastic handle, and a piece of identification that listed him as a freelance employee of the police.

Lulled into a sense of invulnerability over the previous five years, Chikatilo did not think of himself as being in any danger. Either he believed that he had taken all the precautionary measures, or he had faith in his "black hood," or perhaps he trusted his backers, whoever they might be.

What really bothered him were the incidents involving the battery and linoleum. Having documents routinely checked or being stopped on the street for questioning might be annoying, but it was a pretty commonplace occurrence in Soviet Russia, something that almost everyone was subject to at one time or another. But actual criminal charges had been filed against him. The consequences were real, unlike the mere slap on the wrist he might be given for trying to pick up young girls in a train station. In fact, he was on the run from the prosecutor in charge of the case.

That is why, in our opinion, Chikatilo instantly became soaked in sweat when Zanosovsky stopped him near the Central Market and demanded to see his passport.

"It seemed that he recognized me," Zanosovsky testified. "Horror was written on his face, and sweat was streaming down his cheeks. I immediately thought to myself, *This is our man, the one we've been looking for. Murders in Shakhty, and he was registered in Shakhty. Works in Rostov, where there had been one murder after another in Aviators' Park.*" In the police station adjacent to the Market, the suspect's briefcase was opened and searched. The contents only confirmed what Zanosovsky intuitively believed. Chikatilo tried to say something in his defense, but it did not come out very coherently. He was taken to the Pervomaisky police department, where Operation Shelterbelt was being worked on. When everyone else there saw the contents of his briefcase, they too agreed that this was their man.

Now it was time for the regional criminal investigation bureau to carry out a rather painstaking, but obvious, job—checking out Chikatilo's aliases for all the murders then known. This would require a good deal of time, but the suspect could not legally be detained for more than seventy-two hours without being formally accused of something.

Considering the fate of Aleksandr Kravchenko, it should come as no great surprise that such procedural measures are not always strictly followed. An experienced detective or investigator can always think of ways to stretch out a suspect's days behind bars. This time, however, they decided to follow the law. There were more than enough grounds for keeping Chikatilo locked up for as long as the investigation needed.

First, he was charged with harassing women in public places. The most he could get for this was fifteen days, but that would be more than enough time to run a thorough background check on him. Then the detectives received an unexpected break: they uncovered the criminal charges for the theft of state property.

The fact that these were serious charges still under investigation meant that Chikatilo could be kept under guard for weeks, if not months. During this time, all of the suspect's past actions could be scrutinized right down to their smallest details.

The detectives dug into Chikatilo's history, particularly his days as a teacher in Novoshakhtinsk and Shakhty, and found out about the incidents involving the girl in the reservoir and the locked classroom. It had never occurred to anyone at the time that the dirty little acts of a frightened and frustrated middle-aged man were even slightly connected with the series of brutal murders.

Now the detectives gathered information about the ex-teacher in bits and pieces: how his students had considered him a homosexual; how he spied on little girls in the toilet; how he took prostitutes and other "loose" women to a shack he had bought unbeknownst to his family; how he performed—or didn't perform—his duties at Rostovnerud; how he never parted with his briefcase; and how he liked to walk up and down commuter trains from head to rear and back again.

All in all, they were left with the impression of a strange individual. Still, such observations in themselves are insufficient evidence—there are more strange people in the world than there are murderers.

In 1991, when Chikatilo was arrested for the third time—and, for once, with no chance of being let go— prosecutor Issa Kostoyev, after expending a great deal of effort in obtaining the twelve-year-old files of the case, learned for the first time about the body of Lenochka Zakotnova in the Grushevka River. Thanks to Kostoyev, Kravchenko was posthumously acquitted of her murder. Before this, though, other investigators had supposedly dug as far back in Chikatilo's history to 1984, when he was arrested for the first time, but had attached no significance to it.

Finally, Kostoyev would be able to clear up the question of whether Chikatilo could be indicted for the murder of Dima Ptashnikov, a ten-year-old stamp collector who one evening had followed a respectable-looking man to his untimely demise. Everything pointed directly at Chikatilo, with the exception of one detail: the traces of sperm found on the dead boy's body and clothing, after lab analysis, belonged to the fourth type, AB.

A sample of Chikatilo's blood was drawn and taken for analysis, just as a hundred thousand drivers in the Rostov region had been previously checked.

The results were sufficient to drop all charges of murder against him—Chikatilo's blood belonged to the second type. His sperm was never analyzed.

As Viktor Burakov later confessed, they had had no idea then how to get a sample. Could they really have asked a dedicated party member and family man whose guilt was not proven to submit to such a humiliating procedure? There was no reason to analyze his sperm then, a line that was repeated many years later, even after Chikatilo had finally been sentenced.

As it turned out, Chikatilo had beaten incredible odds. His blood type was analyzed as A, but the B antigen is contained in his saliva, sweat, and hair. That is, he really belongs to the fourth type, AB, but the B antigen is not clearly defined in his blood. The chances of this happening are one in twenty thousand. At the time, it was considered axiomatic that a person's blood and sperm must belong to the same group. Only toward the end of 1988 did a medical team from abroad publish its findings about this rare anomaly.

What about the briefcase with its unusual contents? Why would an ordinary supply clerk take along a sharpened knife and rope on a short business trip? It could be argued that he needed them to cut or tie up materials, but someone should have realized that a maniac was being sought in connection with a series of murders in which the victims had often been bound before being stabbed to death. Chikatilo told investigators he used the vaseline for shaving, and the investigators believed him—even though unambiguous marks of sodomy had been found on all the young boy's corpses.

The briefcase, with its material evidence, suddenly vanished into thin air. Many years would pass before any explanation was given. Police lieutenant Marat Urmanchiev, who at the time worked at the Pervomaisky department of internal affairs, stated at the trial that he had personally handed over the briefcase and its contents to the team working on Shelterbelt. The latter, for a reason that no one can figure out, returned the briefcase to the suspect's wife. It was regarded as superfluous to the investigation.

Feodosya Semyonovna accepted the material evidence the detectives no longer needed, and added the well-honed knife to her kitchen utensils.

In spring of 1991, Chikatilo was asked to identify all twenty-three knives in his collection. "Knife number fifteen is very similar in size and shape of blade, as are the color and shape of the handle, to the knife that was confiscated from me and with which I carried out a series of murders. In all probability, I used this knife to kill Luchinskaya, Chepel, Alekseyeva, and Golosovskaya."

G.G. Bondarenko headed the criminal investigation bureau of the Pervomaisky department of internal affairs in 1984. Called to the witness stand in 1991, he instantly recognized knife number fifteen as the one in Chikatilo's briefcase when it was

brought to the Pervomaisky station from the Central
Market.

Meanwhile, Andrei Chikatilo was being held in a
jail cell, awaiting his fate. A decoy was put in the cell
with him in the hope that he would suddenly blurt
out something incriminating in the course of conversation. His new cellmate passed himself off as a
doctor. Medicine was one field in which Chikatilo
showed an inordinate amount of interest. Practically
confessing to rape, he confided to the decoy that
what concerned him most of all was whether or not a
person could hang himself, so to speak, on the results
of a sperm analysis. The latter, naturally, related
everything word for word to the police, but no one
paid him any attention.

For insufficient proof of guilt, Chikatilo should
have been released. Instead, on December 12, 1984,
he was sentenced to one year of correctional labor in
accordance with Article 92 of the Criminal Code of
the Russian Soviet Federated Socialist Republic for
the theft of a car battery. No mention was made of
the linoleum.

He served three months in jail before being
released. He was no longer perceived as a threat to
society.

Jail had been inconvenient, but much worse, to
his way of thinking, was his expulsion from the
Communist Party, whose ideals he had ardently
defended his whole life. It was a cause of great distress. However, perestroika was only a year away
from sweeping through Soviet society at all levels,

and it would not be long before membership in the party was considered more a sad memory than a badge of honor. Chikatilo himself quickly changed his tune in lock-step with the new era, and began cursing all those who had been drumming false propaganda into his head for as long as he could remember.

Perhaps no one was more befuddled about Chikatilo's release than Zanosovsky. He was shocked when he learned that the person he had picked up could not possibly be the same rapist and killer being sought by all the police forces in the region.

His intuition told him otherwise, that he had, in fact, arrested the right man. The experts had to be mistaken. But no one would listen to him. Instead, he was told to get back to his post of staking out the bus station. Soon after, he was relieved of his duties altogether in connection with Operation Shelterbelt for being "overly zealous" in the performance of his duties. It was felt that he might compromise the team's need for conspiracy to keep the killer from feeling he was being shadowed.

Since then, Zanosovsky has continued working as a detective in other divisions and on other cases. Once he and his partner, both weaponless, came upon some armed housebreakers. In the ensuing struggle, his partner was killed and Zanosovky suffered eight stab wounds.

Today he is a prematurely graying man of few words who sadly remembers the year 1984. He believes in the science of criminology, but is just as convinced as ever that a detective's intuition and common sense are his best assets. If these qualities had taken precedence over laboratory analysis, there would have been no need to search another six years for the serial killer.

PART III

"... Condemned to Misery and Woe ..."

CHAPTER 12

Workdays of the Killer, Workdays of the Investigators

1985-1987

ANDREI ROMANOVICH CHIKATILO was released with a clear conscience in mid-December 1984, just in time to celebrate the New Year at home with his family.

He once confessed during the investigation that each New Year was a special occasion for him, a time to tally up the number of victims for the year just gone by, add them to the overall total, and raise a glass to the memory of their souls.

At the trial, public prosecutor N.F. Gerasimenko asked him, "Did you keep track of the number of people you killed?" After a short pause, Chikatilo gave an evasive answer that reflected his passion for military and partisan themes: "I considered them to be enemy aircraft I had shot down." To his way of thinking, shooting down enemy aircraft was not a crime but an act of honor and heroism. It should be mentioned that Chikatilo never erred in his calculations. He knew exactly how many bodies he had lain to waste.

When he was released from prison in 1984, not a trace remained of his former anxieties. He no longer perspired in the presence of uniformed police officers, nor worried about a blood or sperm analysis giving him away. All those fears were behind him now. He had been detained, checked, and released. He was free to continue his murderous rampage.

He rang in the new year at home with his family, and set out in quest of yet another job. There was not even the slightest chance of his returning to Spetsenergoavtomatika. In general, it would be better for him to look outside Rostov. He chose the city of Novocherkassk, halfway between Rostov and Shakhty, where in January 1985 he was hired as chief of the ferrous metals department at an electric locomotive factory. Like his previous two jobs, this one involved travel.

And, as before, he quickly earned a reputation as a poor worker. As usual, he didn't say a word during planning meetings, but stared off into space. Any question posed to him by his director or colleagues interrupted his daydreaming and caught him by surprise. He forgot his assignments or got them confused. Not a day passed in which his bosses didn't give him a good dressing-down, often in the presence of his daughter Lyudmila, who also worked at the factory. One of his coworkers, E.V. Gubernatorov, remembered how Chikatilo bore these attacks in front of his daughter with amazing stoicism, even indifference.

In short, after moving to Novocherkassk, it was clear that Chikatilo's New Year's resolution was not to become a more conscientious employee. However, there was a seemingly contradictory detail about his personality that his colleagues from that period remembered. On the one hand, Chikatilo always forgot what his bosses told him to do, even if he wrote it all down. But on the other, he had excellent recall for where and when he had obtained materials for the factory.

During the investigation he would complain about his poor memory while simultaneously leading investigators to the exact places where he had murdered ten years earlier. In some cases he was off by only a few feet. He also had an excellent memory of his victims—what they looked like, what they were wearing, where he stabbed them and even the degree of pleasure it brought him.

In reality, there was nothing contradictory about Chikatilo's behavior. Anything he was forced to do, like his job, was not worth remembering. Yet he retained a strong memory for the activities that he counted as successful.

His personal habits on the job had not changed any, either. His new colleagues never saw him go out of his way to make contact with anyone. He would politely greet a person in passing, but that was all. He still came to work neatly dressed in a clean shirt and tie. Still, Gubernatorov recalls one detail that Chikatilo's former colleagues in Shakhty and Rostov had not noticed. "He didn't cause any suspicion, but there was something terrible about his smile in profile." It reminded Gubernatorov of a crocodile.

After his three-month stint in jail, Chikatilo didn't kill again for almost a year. His last victim had been Ira Luchinskaya, whose life he had silenced forever in Aviators' Park, not too far from his work and just one week before he was arrested on September 13, 1984.

When he took the job at the locomotive factory, he had counted on business trips to places more interesting than all the same old boring cities nearby. He got his wish toward the end of July, 1985, when he was sent to the Moskabel factory in Moscow.

The trip was a success. He was given a comfortable room in the factory dormitory, he carried out his business affairs without any foul-ups, and he had time on his hands to wander about the capital and do some shopping.

Among the six photographs later shown by investigators to the woman who supervised the dormitory, she immediately recognized the one of Andrei Romanovich. She even remembered his last name because the witness at her wedding had also been a Chikatilo—an incredible coincidence for such an unusual name. She remembered him for another reason: he had asked her to join him after work and go for a walk together.

Fortunately for her, she declined the offer. But she hadn't forgotten the man, who she told the investigators had been very polite and seemed well-educated. At the trial, Chikatilo said that he also remembered the woman. "But I didn't invite her anywhere. And I thank her for the compliment. Her words go to show what kind of man I am." Any flattery was always appreciated. His words implied that if he had invited her for a walk, she would have gone with him.

No matter whose side of the story is correct, the fact remains that Chikatilo had the evening of August 1, 1985 free to himself. He decided to make use of the time by purchasing a plane ticket to Rostov. It is not completely clear why he chose to go to the airport to do this, since there are plenty of ticket offices in the city. He may have thought he stood a better chance of getting a ticket there, or maybe he couldn't resist the temptation to ride a commuter train outside the city.

Experienced Russian travelers know that airplanes to southern cities, including Rostov, leave Moscow from Vnukovo Airport, which is accessible by commuter train. At the time, though, the landing strip at Vnukovo was under repair, and all domestic flights were rerouted from Domodedovo, another Moscow airport, which does have connecting service to and from the trains. This set of circumstances cost eighteen-year-old Nina Pokhlystova her life. She was a mentally retarded girl who enjoyed riding the commuter trains.

"I saw a girl standing on the platform between the cars. She was wearing an old, shabby dress and smoking. I began talking to her. She asked me if I had anything to drink. I answered that I had money and that it wouldn't be a problem to get some vodka. It

was understood that the girl would have sex with me.
We got off at a stop whose name I don't know, passed
a small village, crossed a road, entered a woods and
sat on the grass. She got undressed, and I pulled down
my pants. I wanted to have intercourse with her, but
nothing happened."

What did happen next was the usual, as if he had
not been "out of action" for a whole year. He bound
and strangled her, then stabbed her thirty-eight
times.

Even though he couldn't remember the name of
the station, he later was able to lead investigators to
the precise location in the woods, beyond the village
of Vostryakovo-1, where mushroom pickers found
the decomposed and mutilated corpse under a worn
green raincoat.

Chikatilo returned to the station, and took a train
back to the airport. He did not buy a ticket for the
plane to Rostov, though. Instead, he took a train back
home after spending a number of hours shopping in
downtown Moscow.

Shortly after his return from Moscow—August 27,
to be exact—he ran into eighteen-year-old Inessa
Gulyaeva, a habitual runaway. She had just been
released from a halfway house with orders to return
to her village of Otradnoye at once. She did not want
to take a bus in the evening, but there was no place
for her to spend the night in Shakhty.

A kindly looking man with glasses and gray hair
offered her free lodging for the night. She took him
up on it. He led her only as far as a grove a short dis-

tance from the bus station. She made the mistake of mocking his weakness. That was when he killed her. It was his last murder for 1985.

The next year did not yield any new material for the investigators to work on. No murders bearing the signature of the Rostov maniac were recorded for 1986.

Andrei Romanovich turned fifty years old on October 16, 1986, accepting the congratulations of his family and coworkers. Before he turned fifty-one, he killed three more times.

In early May of 1987 he was sent on a business trip to the small city of Kamensk-Uralsky, southeast of Sverdlovsk (now Yekaterinburg). Ten days into his trip he took a train from Sverdlovsk to the city of Revda—a distance of a few hundred miles—where he had no relatives, no friends, and no business to attend to.

At the Revda train station he encountered Oleg Makarenkov, just three days shy of his thirteenth birthday. He was a student at a boarding school for mentally handicapped children. He hated the school and had asked his parents a number of times to send him elsewhere. On this day, May 16, he had gone by bus with a classmate to school, but had gotten off a few stops earlier, ostensibly to play hookey.

The former teacher did not have a difficult time persuading the boy to go off with him. He invited the boy back to his dacha to enjoy a delicious homemade meal.

Makarenkov was savagely murdered in the woods not far from the train station. After completing his traditional partisan ritual over the disfigured corpse, Chikatilo covered the body with earth and fallen leaves and scattered the boys's shredded clothing along the road. This shelterbelt was not one that mushroom pickers came to often, and in autumn— peak picking time—of that year, no one stumbled upon a dead body.

Chikatilo spent the night in the Revda train station. He left in the morning for Sverdlovsk and from there went to Kamensk-Uralsky. He finished the rest of his business trip and returned home.

On July 29, 1987, Chikatilo set off on another trip, this time to the Ukrainian city of Zaporozhye. At a bus station on the outskirts of town, he spied a young boy sitting near some railroad tracks and smoking. Always ready to trade on his experience as a teacher, Chikatilo began his conversation with twelve-year-old Vanya Bilovetsky on the evils of tobacco. The boy, obviously embarrassed at being caught smoking by a grown-up, threw his cigarette away and headed for home via a path cutting through the woods. Chikatilo followed close behind. He pounced on his unsuspecting victim, whose screams had to be muffled with fistfuls of earth stuffed into his mouth. The only fresh detail to be added to this murder was that police found a knife fragment near the murder site. A piece of metal from the blade had broken off.

During the search of Chikatilo's apartment carried out in 1990, it was revealed that knife number twenty-three had a broken blade. The first thing the Zaporozhye detectives should have done was match up the broken piece with the knife to see if they fit. Unfortunately, they hid the fragment so well that to this day it has not been found.

Chikatilo was dispatched on another trip to Leningrad (now St. Petersburg), where he spent twenty days from September 7-27. About halfway through his stay, he met sixteen-year-old Yura Tereshonek at the Finland train station. The good-natured, outgoing lad studied at one of the local professional schools and lived in the school dormitory. Judging by his shape, Yura was a hearty eater. Chikatilo seduced him with the promise of a meal at his dacha. Yura could not refuse.

They took a train to Lembovo station. *My dacha, he told the boy, is just on the other side of this patch of woods. Dinner is ready. All we have to do is heat it up.* Chikatilo attacked him almost as soon as they entered the woods.

A roster of his murders during his Novocherkassk period, after he had served a three-month jail sentence, reveals the following:

August 1, 1985—Domodedovo, outside Moscow;

August 27, 1985—shelterbelt near the Shakhty bus station;

May 16, 1987—outskirts of Revda, in the Urals;

July 29, 1987—outskirts of Zaporozhye;

September 16, 1987—Lembovo Station, outside
Leningrad.

The half-year hiatus after his release from prison
is easy to explain. Once again he had been miracu-
lously spared. Now he had to exercise caution for
awhile. But what stayed his murderous hand from
August 1985 to May 1987, an interval of almost two
years?

Chikatilo later explained to Kostoyev, when asked
why he had not killed a single time in 1986, that his
colleagues at work had toasted him on the occasion
of his fiftieth birthday and he was, therefore, in a
good mood. But when Kostoyev followed up his question by asking why Chikatilo had gone back to
killing in 1987, and only outside the Rostov region,
Chikatilo had nothing to say. But the next question
brought a surprising response:

Q: Is the reason you did not commit any murders
during this period in Rostov because the police were
closely guarding the commuter trains, bus stations,
and so on?
A: I knew they were looking.

Thus, when the police began to close in, his sense
of caution forced him to go underground and bide his
time for almost two years.

★ ★ ★

In retrospect, it is easy to talk about the errors made by investigators and detectives.

Yet another one, dating to August 28, 1985, involved the corpse of an unidentified woman (later revealed to be Inessa Gulyaeva) discovered near the Shakhty bus station. Among a pile of garbage nearby, a small bundle of women's underwear was found wrapped in a sarafan, a peasant dress. Vladimir Ilyich Kolesnikov, now a general and in charge of the Russian Criminal Investigation Department for all of Russia, but then a colonel and head of the Rostov CID, suspected that the clothes could belong to the dead woman and immediately ordered them taken to forensics for analysis. Later, when the woman's identity was established, the sarafan and underwear were nowhere to be found.

In August of 1984, Vladimir Nikolayevich Kulevatsky, a twenty-seven-year-old truck driver, reported his sister Lyudmila Alekseeva missing. Chikatilo later confessed to her murder on the left bank of the Don, on the eve of his departure for Tashkent. Kulevatsky was immediately placed under suspicion. The investigators tried to pressure him into admitting he had killed his own sister. Eight years later, Kulevatsky was the only immediate family member of a victim to show up every day at Chikatilo's trial.

In the autumn of 1985 Issa M. Kostoyev, then deputy director of the department for violent crime in the prosecutor's office of Russia, took over the case. Fully apprised of the details of Operation

Shelterbelt, he put together a team made up of employees from the Moscow, Kursk, Ulan-Ude, Kirovsko and Rostov police departments, and divided them up into three groups. At the time, he could not have known that the criminal lived and worked in Shakhty but, as far as he was concerned, this dusty mining town was central to the case. He concentrated most of his strength here, under the leadership of Yandiev and Kazakov. The second group worked on the Rostov murders and the third, Novoshakhtinsk, group concerned itself with the less convincing theory of the simpletons.

Kostoyev did not introduce any new techniques into solving the case. All he did was systematize and intensify the routine for searching for the killer, an approach that had been sadly lacking up until then. His underlings began to display greater vigilance in those places where crimes had been committed. From now on, there would be no more cases of material evidence disappearing.

Anyone who had ever been previously convicted of sexually motivated crimes, whether still in jail or set free, was scrupulously checked out, as were the patients of sexual pathologists and venereal disease specialists. Railway workers and soldiers who were assigned to work in track gangs also came under scrutiny. Kostoyev was convinced the man he was looking for was constantly riding the commuter trains. Employees of nightclubs, owners of video equipment and habitues of video salons, especially those where horror films and pornography were shown, as well as former policemen who had been dismissed for improper activities, all fell under Kostoyev's magnifying glass.

One thing Kostoyev was able to do that had been beyond his predecessors' abilities in Rostov was demand—and obtain—information on all analogous murders in the country for the past twenty years. In addition, reports on any and all serious sexual crimes committed just in Russia also passed his desk. By the time Chikatilo committed a murder in Moscow, the investigative team, by examining the killer's signature, was able to determine if the murder was one of "theirs" or did not fit the pattern at all.

Airline ticket stubs were checked, as were airline manifests. Information was gathered on anyone from Rostov staying in a Moscow hotel. No one could have known, or foreseen, that the criminal did not stay in a Moscow hotel but in a factory dormitory, or that he would take a train back to Rostov instead of flying.

Kostoyev sent inquiries to all corners of the country, and regularly received communiques from local bureaus, including from Uzbekistan. But he received no information at all concerning the two murders carried out during Chikatilo's trip to Tashkent. So badly mutilated was the body of the second victim, the girl named Akmaral, that the local militia attributed it to her getting caught in the blades of a harvesting machine.

In December of 1985, Kostoyev and Burakov threw down a net on the commuter trains, from which it should have been impossible for the killer to escape. All trains were to be patrolled by plainclothes police from station to station. One would get off, while another got on, as on a conveyor belt. This procedure continued uninterrupted until June 1986. Policemen and reliable druzhinniki—volunteer militiamen—scoured the area from early morning to early night, checking the faces of the men they saw against the police composite sketch. They checked documents and stopped anyone who looked the slightest bit suspicious. Helicopters overhead patrolled the areas around the suburban train stations and shelterbelts.

Despite all their efforts, Chikatilo avoided falling into their net . . . because he was participating in the manhunt as well! As a freelance employee of the Rostov Department of Internal Affairs, Andrei Chikatilo assisted in patrolling the commuter trains, though he knew he was the object of their search.

This explains why 1986 was an inactive year. By turns cowardly and cautious, he only began killing again in the summer of 1987, and only in places far from where the heat had been turned up high.

★ ★ ★

Chance often plays a role in catching a murderer. But when chance does not intervene, a detective cannot catch the culprit unless he first understands the thought processes and motives of behavior. He must look into the criminal's inner world, no matter how repugnant it might be, and try to see through the killer's eyes.

In an attempt to do so, the investigators invited experts in the field of deviant behavior to come to Rostov and Shakhty and share with them their theories on what kind of person they were dealing with. Psychiatrists and psychologists from the Serbsky Institute, the Institute of Criminology and the Institute of Ministry of Internal Affairs accepted Kostoyev's offer. The leading sexual pathologist of the country, G.S. Vasilchenko, was also in attendance. Each added some detail to the overall portrait of the killer, but the individual who made the greatest contribution was an unknown, self-effacing assistant professor from the provincial Rostov Medical Institute, Aleksandr Bukhanovsky. "It was not I who brought attention to myself," he said later, explaining his popularity in the press. "It was Chikatilo who brought attention to me."

Bukhanovsky drew up two psychological portraits of the criminal. The first, from 1984, gave a fairly accurate description of the man's age and height. His report even had the audacity to call into question the opinions of better-known psychiatrists and criminologists who entertained the notion that there may have been two killers—one killed boys while the other concentrated on girls and women—or even three.

Bukhanovsky was the first person to conclusively lift the veil of suspicion from homosexuals, physicians, and the mentally retarded. In an attempt to shed light on why the killer cut out his victims' organs of sexual reproduction, he stated that it was the result of a horrible combination of sadism, necrosadism, sexual fetishism and vampirism. Others before him had advanced the theory that the killer was a doctor who was motivated by an unholy interest in questions of life and death, or that the killer belonged to a criminal organization that trafficked human organs for transplantation.

His second portrait, drawn up two years later, was amazingly accurate. Only now has it become clear just how accurate, but at the time there was no way to test it. The criminal, as he pictured him, had an asthenic, or weak, build, and suffered either from an inflammation of the prostate gland or from dystonia (Chikatilo was treated in 1984 for the second problem). The scientists from the more prestigious research institutes suggested that the killer was either an unskilled laborer or someone who might have had a professional relationship with a child welfare institute, but once again Bukhanovsky hit the nail right on the head. His criminal would either have a specialized background or a university education with emphasis in the liberal arts and, preferably, would work a regular forty-hour week in industry, perhaps in a supply division.

In his opinion, there was not one Chikatilo, but three persons rolled into one. The first lived a normal life, working and caring for his family and with a fondness for the comforts of home. The second one raped and killed, while the third one—the one who was currently confined to an iron cage—liked to enact the role of someone completely insane.

After Shelterbelt had been brought to a conclusion, Bukhanovsky and his colleagues founded a private treatment and rehabilitation center called "Phoenix," with the goal of rooting out and preventing sexually motivated crimes before they happen, and studying the psychology of people inclined to such behavior—in other words, to cure future Chikatilos from becoming sex-crazed murderers.

* * *

In the meantime, Chikatilo was changing apartments one after the other. In 1986, his family had two two-room apartments in Shakhty; the ill-fated shack on Mezhevoy Lane had long since been sold.

On September 26, 1986, he rented a room in Novocherkassk. In December 1987, Feodosya Semyonovna exchanged one of the Shakhty apartments for a two-room apartment in Novocherkassk.

On June 23, 1988, their daughter Lyudmila Andreyevna traded her Shakhty apartment for another two-room apartment, also in Shakhty. When she divorced her husband and went to live with her parents in Novocherkassk, this apartment remained at her father's disposal. He made use of it.

Finally, on December 27, 1989, Chikatilo once again swapped his daughter's apartment for another and registered it under his wife's name. In order to do so, he had to arrange for a fictitious divorce. A husband and wife are not allowed to have separate apartments in Russia, and divorced couples are viewed as constituting two families.

It is the speed by which he was able to accomplish these apartment maneuvers that is more surprising than anything. His rate of success was quite astonishing, considering that the majority of his countrymen can spend years getting just one apartment.

At his trial, sandwiched between all his ranting and raving about rats in his isolation cell and an Assyrian mafia out to get him, Chikatilo let slip one interesting tidbit of information: he claimed he worked for the KGB. Even though persons much closer to the case and with greater knowledge of its details vehemently deny any such connection between the two, we find it difficult here to dismiss outright Chikatilo's own words.

CHAPTER 13

The Return

1988-1990

HAVING RIDDEN out the storm, Chikatilo emerged once again after investigators, baffled by the almost two-year pause in killings bearing the characteristic signature of the Shelterbelt criminal, concluded that the person—if there was only one—was either dead or had committed suicide from an overwrought conscience. If that were the case, they were not sorry to be rid of him, but on the other hand it would be a bitter reminder of their professional failure and that, in the end, justice had not triumphed.

Kostoyev's and Burakov's people did everything they could. They made the rounds of all the schools, warning teachers, children and parents. In exchange, they gleaned information about suspicious-looking types and incidents, which they followed up right away. Now that the inhabitants of the region clearly knew the dangers, it was supposed that the criminal would think twice about approaching his next victim. Often, if someone spotted a stranger picking up a child in his car, he or she would phone the police or head straightaway to the nearest precinct and report the model, color and license plate number.

231

Blockades on all roads leading out of the city were set up, but again, all such efforts yielded nothing.

The places where the rapist and murderer had left his bloody tracks behind were staked out around the clock. The left bank of the Don and Aviators' Park were under constant surveillance. The fatal stretches of rail between Rostov and Shakhty, where so many mutilated corpses had been found in the shelterbelts not far from the station platforms, were shut down entirely, as were all paths leading to and from them.

Traps were set in the trains and in the stations in the form of young policewomen heavily made up and dressed to look like vagrants, drunks and prostitutes. The killer had shown a predilection for blondes of average height and build. That much was known. What the police did not know was how he was able to lure his victims off the trains or away from the stations into the woods to their untimely and violent end. In effect, the policewomen, who carried nothing more than canisters of mace for self-defense, were risking their own lives. Even though they were being covered at all times by plainclothes officers, there was little that could help them if the murderous beast suddenly appeared out of nowhere, threw them into his car and drove off.

Chikatilo knew all this. He saw all the traps laid out for him, and as a result, he made an unexpected move—he changed his places of murder. He returned to his bloody ways on either the fourth or fifth day of April, 1988—the precise date has never been conclusively established—and murdered an unknown woman in the city of Krasny Sulin.

He had become acquainted with the woman, whose age he estimated at between twenty-five and thirty, in a commuter train. She was on her way to Krasny Sulin, which is beyond Shakhty when traveling from Rostov. Chikatilo followed her and persuaded her to go back to his place. It was still light outside. They walked for about forty minutes until they reached a vacant lot, somewhere in the vicinity of a metals factory. He suggested they sit and rest awhile.

The outcome was the same as it had been so many times before. He propositioned her, and she agreed. He tried to achieve satisfaction the normal way, but nothing happened. The badly disfigured corpse was discovered on April 6. Alongside it, detectives found a footprint belonging to a male, shoe size 9-10. This clue, like all the others before it, turned up nothing.

The locomotive factory in Novocherkassk had sent Chikatilo a number of times to that same metals factory. Thus, he knew where to lead the woman so that no one would see them. He even had the patience to spend forty minutes on setting up his kill. One can only imagine how he must have trembled with anticipation during that whole time, after so many months of self-imposed restraint.

From the chronicle of murders, in which there are intervals of a year or more, it becomes clear that the killer had the will to control his urges for as long as he felt there was danger of being caught—until his sense of invulnerability returned. It seems now that in April 1988 he realized he was no longer the object of the massive search. He once again became convinced of the existence of his "black hood," which protected him from misfortune. His flesh demanded blood.

Little more than a month went by. On May 14, nine-year-old Alyosha Voronko's path crossed that of Andrei Chikatilo. It was the last day of the boy's life.

"I was on a business trip in the city of Artyomovska. I had gone by bus to the station of Nikitovka, and from there by train to the Ilovaisk station. I saw a young boy there. We began talking, and he told me about therapeutic plants. I asked him to show me where they grew . . . I remember stabbing and undressing him. He got away from me. I also remember that I hit him on the head and body with some kind of heavy object. The boy was still half-alive when I had my orgasm."

Artyomovsk is in the Ukrainian region of Lugansk. For the time being, Chikatilo was staying away from the places where he was being sought. After this murder, though, he threw caution to the winds and killed sixteen-year-old Zhenya Muratov exactly two months later, and closer to home.

"In the afternoon, I took the Rostov-Zverevo commuter train to Novocherkassk. I met a boy on the train. He said he had applied to a technical school in Rostov, but was worried about getting accepted. I calmed him down by telling him that I, too, had once graduated from a professional institute. I proposed that we get off at the Leskhoz station and go back to my dacha, where I would help him with his homework. He agreed. We got out and walked in the direction of the village of Donleskhoz . . . I tied his hands with the rope, exposed his chest and began cutting him in the stomach. But before I did that, I first opened his mouth and bit off the end of his tongue, which I swallowed. He died after I had stabbed him. After I had my orgasm, I began to undress him, and untied his hands. I remember Muratov's watch—a big, modern-looking thing with a nice metallic body. I removed it and stomped it into the ground."

Zhenya Muratov was a happy boy who liked to play chess. He was intelligent and sociable. He did not have to be tempted with video films, or dinner, or presents. Still, he could not resist the offer of help from a well-dressed, polite older man. The former teacher had temptations for all kinds of situations.

He had returned and again taken up his methodical killing, with no change in his signature. The police had hoped he had disappeared, or rotted away and died. Now the investigative machinery cranked up again. The latest theory was that the killer had returned to the area after being away from a long time, perhaps as a result of being in a prison camp or a psychiatric hospital.

Anyone who remotely fit these categories was checked and re-checked. The best police forces were conscripted into duty; every directive from the top was followed to the letter. Again, they went from school to school, from station to station, along the highways and railroads. Yandiev, who was in charge of the Rostov group, remembered it as a time when many people working on the case, including himself, threw up their hands at the hopelessness of the situation. Their spirits were at an all-time low. Yandiev even thought about quitting the case more than once. The darkest days in the whole sad history of Operation Shelterbelt were about to begin.

After a brief respite, the killings began again.

The next victim was sixteen-year-old Tatyana Ryzhova, a school dropout and vagrant who was known for entering into casual sexual liaisons. Toward the end of February she was singled out by Chikatilo at the Shakhty train station. He took her back to his daughter's empty apartment. He poured her a shot of vodka and asked her to lie down. The rest proceeded according to the usual scenario.

"After I was convinced she was dead, I wondered what to do with her body. I couldn't find a sled anywhere near the building, but about a block away I found one made of lightweight material. Back in the kitchen I took a table knife and cut off both her legs, and then I decapitated her. I wrapped the legs in the girl's pants and tied it at the top with a string. I wrapped the torso in a fur coat and the head in rags and torn clothing."

The old woman to whom the sled belonged said at the trial that she was also missing some wood. This prompted an indignant outburst from the defendant, who insisted he never stole any wood from her.

Neighbors in the apartment building had heard soul-piercing female screams that evening coming from the daughter's empty apartment. Then there was silence.

Three months later, on May 11, 1989, Chikatilo encountered sixteen-year-old Sasha Dyakonov in downtown Rostov.

"I was walking home from a building supplies store. When I got to Komsomol Square, I saw a young boy ahead of me in his school uniform, holding a briefcase in one hand. I caught up with him. There was no one around. Next to the bridge is a grove . . . The boy was so little that I silently took him by the hand and led him into the grove, just a few feet away from the road. I struck him multiple times with a penknife."

The boy had been so small that Chikatilo had no need to draw on his rich experience acquired over the years as a teacher. He simply led him away into the bushes. The boy's cries for help were drowned out by the passing cars. Chikatilo killed him, cut off his genitals, wrapped them in a bag, and buried it.

"This was the only time that not a single word passed between me and my victim."

On June 20, 1989, Chikatilo found himself in the city of Kolchugino, Vladimirskaya region, where he had been sent on a business trip to the Ordzhonikidze factory. He stayed at a local hotel called "Friendship." At the end of June the days were hot and Chikatilo, not particularly overtaxed with official business, decided to go for a swim in a reservoir just on the outskirts of town. There he saw eleven-year-old Alyosha Makarov. He led him into the woods.

On the following day, two of his coworkers arrived in Kolchugino. They found their boss in a state of extreme drunkenness, something that no one had ever seen before, and not something they would easily forget when asked to testify later. They loaded their car with the materials for the factory and drove back to Novocherkassk, but Chikatilo stayed behind in Kolchugino, returning only on the twenty-fifth.

On August 19, Andrei Romanovich was on his way to visit his parents to celebrate his father's birthday. He still had plenty of time to get to his parents' house.

Yelena Varga, nineteen years old and the mother of a two-year-old son, had been living in Krasnoznamensk while attending school in Novocherkassk. On that day, she had been returning home from school. Chikatilo caught sight of her at a bus stop and offered to accompany her home. He wanted to spring into action right away, but there were people around. Instead, he led her into a wooded area and murdered her. He sliced off part of her face, cut out her uterus and wrapped the pieces in her clothing. This time he was more aroused than usual—it took him a long time to calm down, and he even drove his knife into a tree trunk.

Afterwards, he celebrated his father's birthday.

During the investigation, Chikatilo was asked if he had ever received any special medical training.

Forensic analysis of the victims' bodies had determined that the killer was quite adept at pinpointing
specific organs and quickly removing them. He
replied that he did not have any specific training, but
that medicine was a branch of knowledge that interested him and that he had an approximate idea of
where everything in the body is located. He said the
uterus was easy to find because of its bright red color.

On August 28, he came upon ten-year-old Alyosha
Khobotov standing near a video salon on the corner
of Soviet and Karl Marx Streets in Rostov.

"Khobotov took me up on my offer to go back to
my place and watch a film. I thought about taking
him to the cemetery . . . Around about 1987 or 1988 I
had dug myself a grave in the city's main cemetery."

Chikatilo confessed to the murder of Alyosha
Khobotov during his interrogation, although it had
not been one of the murders originally attributed to
him. He led investigators to the cemetery and
showed them where he had dug his grave. Under a
layer of earth, they found the boy's remains and rot-
ting clothes. He also told the investigators that
whenever his conscience bothered him, he would
come to this cemetery.

Alyosha's mother went in search of her son on her
own, after getting no help from the police. She
rushed from one commuter train to another, waving
a photograph of her missing son.

On one of those trains, she actually met her son's
murderer face to face. Feodosya Semyonovna, who
was with Chikatilo at the time, grabbed her husband

by the hand and led him out of the car. There are witnesses who can corroborate this. People who are convinced she knew of her husband's crimes point to this incident on the train as proof. That seems unlikely, however, given Feodosya's genuine despair when she found out about the charges against Chikatilo.

Moreover, the murder of young boys did not square with the love she had always been certain of that he felt toward their grandson. In view of the almost complete absence of any sex life at home, it would have been inconceivable to her that her husband was capable of committing brutal, sexually motivated crimes.

She recalled during questioning that she had sometimes noticed spots of blood on his clothing, but his explanations had always seemed believable. At the factory it was easy to get nicked and cut from loading and unloading supplies. Besides, if she knew what he had been up to all these years or was a willing accomplice, why would she tell investigators about these traces of blood?

Alyosha Khobotov was Chikatilo's last victim in 1989. He did not kill again until the following January. In the meantime he continued to make passes at women, but that was as far as it went.

The chain of killings had snapped for two reasons. First, he was experiencing more problems at work and once again feuding with his superiors, whom he felt, as usual, did not properly appreciate him. Thus, his mind was occupied with leaving the factory and moving on to a new job.

The second reason had to do with problems closer to home. A public toilet was being erected under the windows of the apartment where he and his wife, even though they were supposedly divorced, usually lived. That was bad enough, but to make matters even worse, his neighbors decided to build coopera-tive garages practically right next door. He could put up with the toilet, but the garages made him snap. He began writing letters of complaint to one office after another. At first his letters were polite, sprin-kled here and there with revolutionary rhetoric like "I'll erect barricades [against their garages]."

He sent his letters of complaint by registered mail first to the regional party committee, then the Central Committee of the Communist Party, and finally to Mikhail Gorbachev himself, then General Secretary of the Party. The flowery prose of his let-ters was of no use. Chikatilo became angry at the whole world, but especially at peoples from the Caucasus—the neighbors involved in building the garages were either Armenian or Azerbaidzhani. In his next letter he railed against an Armenian mafia, replaced in subsequent letters by Azerbaidzhani, Abkhazian, and Assyrian mafias. By the time of the trial, they had all been transformed into the Abyssinian mafia. He was also convinced that this Assyrian mafia was following him, and trying to run him down in one of their cars.

Occupied in his battle with "the mafia," Chikatilo's activities on the sexual front abated somewhat. The year 1989 ended for him in woes and worries. In the beginning of January, Chikatilo was hired at an electric locomotive plant in Rostov, not far from the central train station where he had been followed by Captain Zanosovsky before being arrested for the first time. Once again, he ended up in the supplies division.

1990 was to be his final year of freedom. His new job lasted less than ten months. In November he was arrested, but in the period between January and November he murdered nine more times.

His targets of choice had by then switched to young boys. Of his next eight victims, seven were boys ranging in age from seven to sixteen. Chikatilo lured them into Rostov's Botanical Gardens or the shelterbelt near Leskhoz station with his usual array of promises and temptations.

The body of the last boy, sixteen-year-old Vadim Tishchenko, was found on November 3 near the Kirpichnaya station platform. Investigators insisted that just a few days before the station had been under heavy guard. What they did not know was that the patrol had been removed in the days since due to a lack of manpower in Novocherkassk. Once again, Chikatilo had slipped in under their net.

In the final three weeks between then and Chikatilo's arrest, Yandiev was in a state of agitation, but this time he was not despairing. On the contrary, he now had the premonition that he would soon meet up with the criminal. His gut told him that the horrible twelve-year nightmare would soon be over. He called Kostoyev in Moscow and told him to come to Rostov right away. Together, they laid out a plan.

All train stations and bus stops were put under massive, round-the-clock surveillance. For the first time during the operation, the police were equipped with special night vision goggles. The commuter trains were put under constant patrol, just as they had been a few years earlier. Young, blonde police-women of average height and build, in accordance with the killer's tastes, once again dressed provoca-tively and rode the trains from one end of the region to the other.

Chikatilo was probably aware of all these mea-sures, but, if he was, he did not go into hiding as he normally did under such circumstances. Instead, he continued to act right out in the open. For example, there was the incident with I.P. Belova, a vocational school student. He had spotted her on the train from Novocherkassk to Shakhty. Sitting next to her, he placed his hand on her knee. When the girl made it known to him that she found his behavior offensive, he responded, according to Belova, "What, you don't like it? Women used to like it before." Chikatilo told her he had missed his stop, but would travel with her to Shakhty, where they got out together. He then offered to walk her home and carry her bag. Belova agreed to let him accompany her home, deliberately choosing a path where she knew there would be many people around. He asked her out to the movies

that evening, and said he would wait for her outside
while she got her mother's permission. She declined
the offer. Later she said she had not been afraid of the
man, who, except for his hand on her knee, acted
very gentlemanly toward her and claimed he was a
teacher.

She had unwittingly looked death in the face
without suspecting a thing. She told no one,
including her mother, about her meeting with the
man. Later she was able to recognize him instantly.

Fatigued and soaked from the never-ending
autumn rains, Yandiev and his constant companion
in those days, Ivan Vasilyevich Vorobyinsky, slogged
on in search of new witnesses. They questioned one
ticket seller after another at all the train stations
until finally they came upon a woman who remembered selling a ticket to Vadim Tishchenko on what
would be the last day of his life. The ticket stub was
found among shreds of clothing near the corpse.

The attendant, L.A. Prishcheva, who sold tickets
from the first window at the Shakhty station, recognized the boy from a photograph. She remembered
taking a ten-ruble note from him and giving him
back four rubles in change. Upon further questioning,
Prischeva said she had seen a tall man with glasses
standing near the ticket window. As she described his
features, Yandiev's heart began to beat faster.

For the first time they had a fresh clue—a witness
who had actually seen the alleged criminal and his
victim together a few hours before the crime.
Prishcheva also mentioned that her daughter had told

her something about a man she had seen in a train about a year ago trying to talk a boy into getting off at one of the stations with him. The boy had run away from him.

Yandiev and Vorobyinsky asked permission to meet the daughter, Svetlana Naprasnikova. She had been one of a group of girls sitting next to the boy when the man had approached him. Svetlana not only described the man's appearance in detail, but added that she had often seen him on the trains.

Now it was only a question of when Chikatilo would be arrested. That would occur two weeks later, but not before he would claim one more victim.

CHAPTER 14

The Final Victim

1990

CHIKATILO'S FINAL victim was twenty-two-year-old
Svetlana Korostik. He took her to one of his favorite
killing grounds, the shelterbelt near the Leskhoz station platform, on November 6, 1990—exactly two
weeks before his arrest.

She had turned out to be easily approachable, and
had agreed to lie down with him in the grass. As
always, he could not perform, and murdered her. He
swallowed the tip of her tongue and her nipples,
throwing away everything else that he had cut off
after she was dead. He covered the body with earth
and leaves. The knife used on her, designated as
number twenty, had also been used for killing three
boys. As he emerged from the woods afterward, three
or four women, who had been in the same area earlier
looking for mushrooms, were standing near the platform. So was Sergeant Igor Rybakov of the police,
assigned to Operation Shelterbelt.

On this wet and rainy day, he was patrolling the
Leskhoz station on his own, because his partner had
failed to show. Instructions had been to patrol only in
pairs but no one would know if an officer broke the
rules. Still, Sergeant Rybakov had not willfully vio-

lated them, and in general was conscientious about performing his duties. The absence of his partner put him in an uncomfortable position.

Dressed in uniform, Rybakov was sitting off a little to the side from the platform, near a little campfire that the women had set while waiting for their train to come. He looked at his watch—his shift would soon be coming to an end. He was thinking about getting his things ready to go when he saw a tall man, dressed in a coat and peaked cap, a bag slung over his shoulder, coming out of the woods. Rybakov's initial impression was that he was just another mushroom picker. But there was something about the man's appearance that put the sergeant on guard. It was the bag. A person would have to be out of his mind to put mushrooms in a soft bag like that. They would get moldy inside. What would someone be doing in the woods on a rainy day, if not looking for mushrooms?

The man in the cap walked along the railway bed and disappeared behind the ticket window. Rybakov debated whether or not to go after him, but the man suddenly reappeared, crossed the tracks and casually approached the campfire. He was hunched over, wiping his perspiring cheeks as he walked.

He walked up to the group of women, exchanged greetings with them, and asked if they had gathered a lot of mushrooms. One of the women pointed to the half-empty basket, while another jokingly answered, "It's not much, but at least it's ours. What kind of luck did you have?" The man smiled a bit crookedly and shrugged, as if to say, *What kind of mushrooms are there in weather like this?*

Rybakov could not take his eyes off the man's clothing. Strictly speaking, there was nothing especially unusual about it, except for the small branches and leaves stuck to his back. That made sense, but his shoes were clean, as if they had just been washed off. One more detail caught his eye: there was blood on his cheek and earlobe, and one of the fingers on his right hand was bandaged.

Rybakov stood up and took a few steps forward. The stoop-shouldered man continued talking with the women.

"Citizen!" Rybakov called to him.

The man shuddered and turned around. Rybakov motioned him over with his finger, and showed him his identification. He asked the man to produce his documents. Rybakov observed the man carefully as he dug through his pocket, noticed the circles under his eyes, the grayish stubble on his face, the dirty bandage on his finger, and the yellowish smear on his cheek. The man, while pulling out his documents, avoided looking Rybakov in the face the whole time.

In between his passport and a card listing the stranger as a senior engineer at the Rostov electric locomotive repair factory, there was one other piece of identification, a special railroad pass that gave him the right to travel for free on the commuter trains. Rybakov's heart skipped a beat—one of the theories was that the killer they were looking for could be a railway worker.

In the distance, the green light of an approaching train could be made out through the mist. As if trying to make the sergeant understand that he did not want to miss the oncoming train, Chikatilo glanced in the direction of the platform.

Rybakov knew he should ask the man specific questions, but he was suddenly tongue-tied. He managed to inquire what the man was doing here on a workday and where he was going.

The man self-assuredly replied that he was going to Rostov, that he had taken the day off from work to see a friend in Shakhty in the morning. Afterwards, he had decided to take a walk in the woods for some fresh air. He impatiently pushed back the sleeve of his jacket and tapped his watch as the train neared the station. "You can go," said the sergeant.

Chikatilo disappeared behind the doors of the train, leaving Rybakov standing there with his doubts. He wanted to jump on the train himself, but the automatic doors closed, and the train pulled smoothly away from the platform. As the rear of the train vanished in the haze, Rybakov stood on the empty platform and repeated to himself the man's strange last name: Chikatilo.

He crossed the tracks and asked a couple of young boys standing near the ticket window if they had seen a tall man with a bag. He was just here, they told him, washing his shoes and hands under a water fountain.

Rybakov reported to his superiors about the man he had stopped and checked. Intuition told the sergeant that this individual was guilty of something, but he had no idea that he had personally stopped the man police had been searching twelve years for. Sergeant Rybakov was later awarded a substantial bonus for his assistance in Chikatilo's arrest.

★ ★ ★

On November 6, 1990, the trains were running behind schedule. As a result, the posting of a police guard at the Lesostep station on the stretch of rail between Novocherkassk and Krasny Sulin was switched from its normal time and moved up to after ten-thirty in the morning.

Chikatilo had stepped off the train with Svetlana Korostik at the Lesostep station before ten-thirty. After the murder, he tramped through the woods to the neighboring station of Leskhoz where Sergeant Rybakov had been on duty. If the post had been in place from the morning on, it is certain the police would have spotted a man, accompanied by a woman in tattered clothing, disappearing into the woods. Korostik might still be alive.

The twelve long years between his first murder and his last were coming to an end. Only fourteen days remained before it would all be over.

On November 6, the investigators gathered for one of their late evening briefings to go over all the names of the individuals that had been detained in the area that day. The name Chikatilo was not among them.

Exactly one week later, General Gerasimov was on his way to inspect the murder site of Vadim Tishchenko. It was pouring rain, and the general had to force himself to get out of his car. Near a pole with a red flag on it to mark the spot, he caught sight of something that looked like a jacket lapel on the ground. Since the other police officers had told him when he arrived on the scene that all the material evidence had already been gathered, he angrily ordered them to fan out over a radius of a quarter mile and comb the area once again. Before half an hour had passed, the body and clothing of Korostik turned up. It was then that the head of the Krasny Sulin police department fished out a piece of paper with the name of one other person who had been stopped in the last few days—Chikatilo.

Investigator Kostoyev was furious when he learned that the man had been let go. "Are you working or sleeping?" he screamed at the police. They replied that the man had already checked out in their records.

Kostoyev had to drum into their heads that blood and sperm analyses were not enough to acquit a person, especially since they had been informed in 1988 that anomalies in the results, however rare, nonetheless existed. A person's physiology was also not enough to go on because, again, the experts could be wrong. What was absolutely necessary was to ascertain where the person had been at the time a murder was committed.

Kostoyev ordered Yandiev to fix Chikatilo's whereabouts on May 14, 1988, the day Alyosha Voronko was murdered in Ilovaisk. Records from his former job showed that Chikatilo had been on a business trip that day in the same city. Everything matched up. Kostoyev decided to take him right away, but the police suggested a different plan. They would follow the man until they caught him in the act. The next time he took a victim into the woods, they would be right behind him. Naturally, there was some risk involved, but if the police were on their toes, they'd nab him before he could do anything. Kostoyev and Yandiev debated the various plans, before concluding that they could wait no longer. They chose November 20 as the day to make their move.

Tuesday, November 20, was foggy and rainy, with even the first few snowflakes of the season mixed in. Chikatilo was at his job. His finger was still aching from one of his adolescent victims who had offered some resistance and bitten him, hard, three weeks earlier. It hurt more with each passing day. He couldn't do anything around the house, and at work he couldn't even hold a pen properly. Unable to suffer the pain any longer, he left work and dropped in at a nearby clinic, where x-rays revealed that the finger was broken. Chikatilo was given a shot to alleviate the pain, and the finger was re-wrapped and put in a cast.

He went home. His wife Fenya was still at work. Rummaging about in the refrigerator, he found some leftovers and ate them cold. After he had eaten, he felt like washing the food down with some beer. Grabbing his three-liter can, with the intention of only filling it halfway, he headed out to the street. On the stairs, he suddenly remembered that he had left his wallet at home.

Before returning home, Chikatilo spotted a young boy in a muddied jacket. He went up to him, but quickly walked away as an old woman approached them. She passed. He spotted another boy and began talking to him, but at that moment the boy was called home.

An unmarked police car pulled up nearby. The time was exactly three-forty in the afternoon. Three men dressed in leather jackets and jeans got out of the car and approached Chikatilo from the front. Two more came up from behind and closed right in on him to prevent him from moving.

"Chikatilo, Andrei Romanovich? You're under arrest."

The handcuffs clicked shut. The men took their prisoner by the arm and led him to the waiting car. The whole scene, and the few minutes preceding it when he had engaged the two young boys in conversation, had been captured by another officer on videotape.

CHAPTER 15

Under Escort

AS HIS HANDS were being cuffed behind him, Chikatilo did not say a word, nor make any attempt to resist. His silence continued in the car, giving the arresting officers the feeling that the man was completely disinterested in everything around him, even as to why he had been literally picked off the street in broad daylight.

Finally, when he did speak, his first words were, "This just goes to show once again that it doesn't pay to argue with the boss." A little while later, he said, to no one in particular, "Still, all things considered, you can't argue with the boss." After that, he did not utter another word for the rest of the ride.

He was taken directly to the office of Mikhail Grigorevich Fetisov, head of the regional Department of Internal Affairs. Kostoyev and his deputy, the head of forensic medicine, and others were waiting for him as well.

In response to the first formal questions regarding name, age, place of residence and place of work, Chikatilo mumbled, stuttered, and forgot even the simplest words. He could not remember where he worked, and he had great difficulty stating the date of his marriage. In addition, in what could have been interpreted as a nervous reaction, he kept yawning.

Many months later, after a painstaking investigation that involved questioning hundreds of witnesses, confrontations between the suspect and individuals from his past, "field trips" to all the murder sites around the country, and one-on-one conversations with the man, Amurkhan Yandiev would eventually come to the shocking and unlikely conclusion that the rapist and murderer, who had terrorized a region of four million people and whose arrest had required the skills and efforts of the best-trained members of the police forces and detective squads, was a coward.

But no one knew that in November 1990. In their minds, the investigators were dealing with an extremely dangerous criminal, the likes of which the world had rarely known. When he was arrested, a search of his briefcase revealed the same contents as six years earlier when he was picked up for the first time by Zanosovsky and Akhmatkhanov. From this, the investigators could only conclude that Chikatilo had left the house that day for more than just beer.

* * *

After his initial deposition was recorded and his mug shots had been taken, Chikatilo was put in a KGB isolation cell. The choice seemed unusual, even though it was considered the most reliable kind of cell for preventing escapes. Yet, everything to that point about the suspect's behavior suggested that escaping was the last thing on his mind. A KGB isolation cell is clean and rather comfortable, relatively speaking. A prisoner is given a cot instead of a plank bed to sleep on, plus his own sink and toilet. Even the food is better than in regular prison. Referring to his cell, Chikatilo liked to joke that it was "his little resort."

A search of his apartment turned up twenty-three knives, a hammer, a pair of shoes, from which investigators had taken a footprint in the past near one of his victim's bodies, and all his clothing.

★ ★ ★

He was given a cellmate who claimed he had been arrested for embezzling a huge sum of money. It has to be assumed that the man was a plant. During the investigation and trial that followed, Chikatilo's cellmates were changed on a regular basis, but it appears he gave them very little information to pass on, unlike the first time he spent in jail, when he had wondered aloud to his partner if sperm could be proof of guilt.

This time, he was more cunning. What he feared most of all was that the other prisoners would find out who he was and what his crimes were, and take the law into their own hands.

Once, during the trial, he said, "I've come here to my own funeral. Let's get it over with quickly. I want to die." Either it was a momentary lapse of weakness on his part, or a cleverly concealed act. Chikatilo wanted to live. When he was taken around the country from city to city to re-enact the scenes of his crimes, he asked the group of investigators escorting him to give him a fictitious name, along with a fictitious charge—grand larceny, for example—whenever he was put in a jail cell with someone else.

In Shakhty he was held in a temporary isolation cell under a pseudonym. The only person who knew his true identity was the warden, but that did nothing to ease his anxieties. "I lived a long time in this city," he said. "If the rumor gets around that I'm here, I'm dead." He asked to be addressed as Nikolai Ivanovich. Whenever his escort had to take him by plane to visit the more remote sights of his killings, such as Tashkent, he tried to conceal the fact he was wearing handcuffs. This was not done out of shame, but from fear that people would recognize him and kill him.

The interrogation began the day after his arrest. Kostoyev was in charge, and for the first part of it he did not let anyone else near the suspect. It was important to make that first contact, win the prisoner's trust and smooth the way for further questioning.

Kostoyev had managed to study Chikatilo's life story to the point where he probably knew it just as well, if not better, than Chikatilo himself. His questions hit the mark, but Chikatilo refused to confess to anything. Instead, he maintained that he had not committed any murders, had already done time for the theft of a car battery—even though he was innocent of the charge, he had hastened to add—and had already been checked in the past for suspicion of murder and been given a clean bill of sale. As far as he was concerned, this was just another example of the persecution he had put up with all his life.

He wrote an official letter of protest to the prosecutor, in which he stated, "I believe that the investigative bodies are prosecuting me because I sent letters of complaint to various courts about the unlawful activities of individuals in the city of Shakhty, who tried to build cooperative garages in the courtyard of the building in which my son lives."

After handing this statement to Kostoyev, Chikatilo refused to answer any more questions. Two days later, Chikatilo gave him a new statement, addressed to the Prosecutor General of Russia: "I felt a kind of madness and ungovernability in perverted sexual acts. I couldn't control my actions, because from childhood I was unable to realize myself as a real man and a complete human being." It was the closest he had come thus far to making a confession, but the statement was still too vaguely worded to be of any real consequence. His first real confession, though not about any murders, came on November 27, when he told Kostoyev about the incidents involving his former students. The following day he wrote another letter to the Prosecutor General that gave some insight into his mind:

"My inconsistent behavior should not be misconstrued as an attempt to avoid responsibility for any acts I have committed. One could argue that even after my arrest, I was not fully aware of their dangerous and serious nature. My case is peculiar to me alone. It is not fear of responsibility that makes me act this way, but my inner psychic and nervous tension. I am prepared to give testimony about the crimes, but please do not torment me with their details, for my psyche would not be able to bear it. It never even entered my mind to conceal anything from the investigation. Everything which I have done makes me shudder. I only feel gratitude toward the investigating bodies for having captured me."

Not long after this statement, Chikatilo would relate all the details of his crimes in coldblooded, emotionless language. His fragile psyche would hold up under questioning, too.

Kostoyev first started to unravel the murder of Alyosha Voronko in Ilovaisk while Chikatilo was in the area on official business. All the circumstances matched up to such a degree that it had to be more than just coincidence. But Chikatilo held his ground—he didn't know anything, he hadn't seen anything, and he hadn't been there. It was clear to the investigator he was blatantly lying.

Chikatilo had already been recognized by some girls who had seen him bothering a boy in a train. He was also recognized as the man standing near Vadim Tishchenko beside a ticket window at the Leskhoz station. On the other hand, he had already been excluded from the list of suspects because of the falsely construed analysis of his blood and sperm samples. The most compelling evidence of all, though, for potentially dismissing him as the killer, was that not a single soul had seen him kill, and not a single person had lived to tell how he used his knives to strike the lethal blows. No one even saw him enter a wooded area with a victim, and emerge from on it alone.

As far as the knives were concerned, they were damaging, but not conclusive, evidence. Experts cannot say with absolute certainty whether certain murders were committed with specific knives. They can only infer that a specific knife could have been used to commit a certain murder, based on the nature of the stab wounds.

While the investigation continued, Chikatilo made use of his time by writing a few more letters of complaint, in which he repeated his assertion that the charges he had been accused of were all trumped-up. Then he lapsed into silence, refusing to answer another question.

On November 29, eight days after Kostoyev had asked the first questions of the interrogation, which clearly was going nowhere, a car was sent early in the morning from the Department of Internal Affairs to pick up Dr. Bukhanovsky at his office. No explanation was given as to why. Only when he arrived there was he filled in for the first time on all the details of the investigation thus far. He was told by the investigators that they were interrogating a suspect. They were certain he was the man they had been searching for in connection with the series of sexually motivated crimes, but they had yet to make any serious headway in cracking him.

Bukhanovsky agreed to speak with the prisoner, but only on his own terms. He was a physician, he reminded Yandiev, and not a detective. Therefore, the notes he took and the tapes he made were to be for his use only and not to be used as evidence against Chikatilo. The man's history was a complete blank to the doctor, even though he had submitted accurate profiles of the hypothetical killer to the investigation in the past.

The first thing Bukhanovsky told Chikatilo was that he considered everything that had happened to be the result of a mental disorder. He assured Chikatilo he would try to explain the mechanism of his mental breakdown to the court, and he also promised that he would explain everything about him to his family. Bukhanovsky was later present when Chikatilo broke down in genuine tears when he received his first note from his wife on November 30.

Yandiev was responsible for arranging a meeting between Chikatilo and Feodosya Semyonovna. When she found out where her husband was and what he had been charged with, she refused to go. Eventually he convinced her to change her mind. As soon as Chikatilo saw his wife, he immediately averted his eyes. "How could you, Andrei?" were the only words she could think to say. His eyes still glued to the floor, he mumbled, "Fenochka, I didn't listen to you. You told me to get treatment, but I didn't listen to you." Yandiev got them to sit down together and asked her to speak to him about their son. It was important that he not forget he was still a father and husband, in spite of everything that had happened.

Chikatilo and Bukhanovsky spent almost the entire day of November 30 in conversation, during which Chikatilo began to speak aloud for the first time about the horrible deeds that lay on his conscious. Bukhanovsky was left with the impression that his partner had just dropped a great burden from his shoulders, and now was ready to confess at great length.

The next day, following his conversation with the psychiatrist, Chikatilo began to open up to the investigative team. He told them everything in great detail, concealing virtually nothing. Whenever he did attempt to cover up something, his interrogators were nonetheless able to draw the information out of him.

Over a period of six days, beginning November 30 and continuing through December 5, Chikatilo unburdened his soul of thirty-four of the thirty-six murders he had been charged with. The other two have since been solved.

At first reluctant, Chikatilo finally admitted to the sexual nature of his crimes. Under the pressure of Kostoyev's questioning, he yielded one detail after another. He claimed that he roamed like "a poisoned wolf" in search of his victims, with no regard for age or appearance. Still, there was a certain amount of craft in his performance. While confessing the crimes, he would still try to find ways to justify his evolution from a sordid pervert to a full-fledged killer. The way he saw it, if it had not been for the police letting him go in 1978 after the murder of Lena Zakotnova, he never would have been free to kill again.

With each new day, he began to confess to more murders. By the time he was finished, eighteen more victims had been added to the original thirty-four, making a grand total of fifty-two. A few months later, in spring 1991, during the period of the investigation when he was leading the escort from one murder site to another with uncanny accuracy, he suddenly remembered his fifty-third victim, twenty-year-old Sarmite Tsany, a Latvian girl he had met in July 1984. He also remembered which knife he had used on her.

Before his case could go to court, Chikatilo still had to undergo a battery of psychiatric tests at the Serbsky Institute in Moscow to determine whether or not he had been in his right mind when he murdered. This was the same infamous Serbsky Institute that had gained worldwide opprobrium during the Brezhnev years for locking up dissidents and other nonconformists to the Soviet system on the pretext they were mentally ill. The formula had been quite simple: If a person was living in the best and most democratic country in the world, the Soviet Union, there would be no reason to complain. Ergo, he must be suffering from some psychic disorder.

Chikatilo spent the fall of 1991 in Moscow as he submitted to a series of tests lasting for two months. Once again, he was at the center of attention, just as he had been when leading the investigators around the country and demonstrating on a dummy his methods of killing. This seemed to give him much greater pleasure than the prospect of actually being cured of his illness. He was very cooperative and polite, not at all the maniac everyone had been expecting.

After passing a whole series of tests and experiments, interviews and analyses, a team of six psychiatrists, led by Andrei Tkachenko, concluded he was of sound mind, accountable for his actions, and able to stand trial.

CHAPTER 16

In the Cage

APRIL 14–OCTOBER 15, 1992

THE TRIAL OPENED on April 14, 1992. Shortly before ten in the morning, Yelena Georgievna Khramova, secretary to Judge Akubzhanov, stood before the entrance to courtroom number five and responded in a hushed voice to questions from the families of the victims and journalists. The atmosphere was charged with tension. No one knew what to expect on the other side of the doors.

At exactly ten o'clock, everyone was invited to step into the room. Almost immediately, the solemnity of the occasion was shattered by the clank of a bolt being moved back, followed by the thud of footsteps coming up the stairs. The first face to be seen emerging from the basement of the Rostov Regional Court was that of Andrei Chikatilo.

It was a moment of "firsts." The first ones among the public to set eyes on him were the families of the victims—the mothers, fathers, brothers and sisters. One of the women took a step toward the cage, where the prisoner now sat, and stopped short, falling to the ground. It was the first fainting session of the trial, and the first time that medics on hand had to administer first aid.

And for the first time, Leonid Akubzhanov, a no-nonsense judge with fourteen years' experience behind the bench, entered the courtroom and took his seat. He was accompanied by his two helpers, the so-called assessors, Aleksandr Levo, a bus driver, and Vladimir Aleksandrov, a factory worker.

Court had been called to order; the trial had begun. The judge spent the first two days reading out the indictment against the defendant Chikatilo. The room acoustics were terrible, and on top of that the judge had poor diction. Even from the third row, it was difficult to make out his words.

On the next day, Chikatilo countered by announcing that he had not been given proper time to acquaint himself with the charges lodged against him, and threatened a hunger strike. Anyone who had ever seen him eat with his usual gusto knew that it was a ruse.

When the judge had finished reading the long indictment, he declared that he was conducting an open trial, for the benefit of journalists. "There will be no secrets," he said. "Let this trial at least teach us something so that this will never happen anytime or anywhere again." The defendant's name, hitherto referred to in the press only as "Citizen Ch.," was now considered to be public information. "Let us finally begin to call everything by its real name," he concluded, a reference to the decades of silent repression upon which the Soviet people had been weaned.

Unfortunately, the journalists, not used to this kind of thing, went a bit overboard at the judge's suggestion, calling the defendant not only by his real name, but—far worse—branding him as the murderer long before the court had passed sentence.

On April 16, Akubzhanov extended Chikatilo the courtesy to "pour out his soul in a kind of freeform short story." Chikatilo seized upon the opportunity, and for the next two hours droned on in a flat, monotonous voice. The longer he spoke, the more it seemed obvious that he was simulating insanity. More and more bits of utter nonsense entered his speech. It had been a mistake to let him speak.

From that point on, he began interrupting the judge whenever the latter tried to intervene, complained about the radiation and rats in his isolation cell, pulled down his pants in front of the public at every available opportunity, and sang the socialist anthem, "The Internationale."

After his scenes were over, he was led back down to his basement cell where he played chess with his partner, read newspapers, ate a good meal, and slept undisturbed until the morning. This information was provided to the authors of this book by reliable and informed sources. His chess partner once let slip, "If you knew what kind of person he was, you'd strangle him with your own hands."

Meanwhile, after he had unburdened his soul in his "freeform short story," Chikatilo was asked various questions, some of which are reproduced below:

Q: Why did you carry vaseline around with you?

A: To use as shaving cream.

Q: Why did you prefer young boys?

A: It made no difference. I asked out women with whom I worked.

Q: What did you do with the victims' severed organs?

A: I threw them on the road, stomped on them, mixed them in with the dirt—I wasn't thinking about anything.

Q: What did you do with the money, watches, and jewelry?

A: (indignant) I threw them away, of course, or crushed them on the ground. In general, I don't remember.

Q: Did you ever think of the pain you were causing your victims? When you were killing boys, didn't you ever stop to think of your own son?

A: It never entered my mind.

Judge Akubzhanov, a strict individual who often spoke his mind without thinking through the consequences, would shout back at the defendant, "Don't do us any favors, Chikatilo, just answer the questions!" or "Shut your mouth, Chikatilo, or they'll write about you that you're crazy. You're not crazy!"

Outbursts such as this led the defense to point out the accusatory nature of the trial and the partiality of the court. By the time, ten days later, that Akubzhanov finally got around to publicly upbraiding the journalists for prematurely convicting

Chikatilo of murder in the press, it was already too late.

The first real sensational trial moment occurred on April 21 when Chikatilo, in the middle of one of his rambling monologues, unexpectedly exclaimed that he had not killed Lena Zakotnova, and that the investigators had accused him "wholesale" for all the murders they didn't have answers for. He had simply signed what they wanted.

The judge had to remind him of the circumstances of the crime to which he had voluntarily confessed, and of such details as the girl's eyes being blindfolded by a scarf, something that no one other than he, the defendant, could have known.

From April 21-24, the judge interrogated him on every crime, bur Chikatilo declined to answer a single question. His lawyer, Marat Khabibulov, asked the court to allow Dr. Bukhanovsky to take part in the trial and help the court, as he was the only competent person who could exert any kind of influence on his client. The request was denied. Once again, Chikatilo threatened to go on a hunger strike.

On April 27, Judge Akubzhanov made a decision not to interrogate Chikatilo on individual episodes, if he was so adamant about not answering. He decided, instead, to let the prosecution, the defense, and the families of the victims ask the questions. The following exchange is an excerpt from that session:

Prosecutor N.F. Gerasimenko: Was the prelimi-
nary investigation, in your opinion, carried out objec-
tively?

Chikatilo: Yes.

G: After 1978, did you work for the police?

C: Yes.

G: Defendant, what happened to those "Zarya"
and "Raketa" watches that formerly belonged to your
victims?

A: Maybe I'm also supposed to remember if they
had crabs or not?

G: Why did you spy on little girls in the toilet?

A: Ask the doctors. They have everything written
down about me. It's also written there that I kept my
hands in my pants all day long, stroking it from
morning till night.

The court sessions for April 28 and 29 were barred to
the public and the journalists. Chikatilo announced
during these session that he was no longer going to
provide any more testimony, insofar as the judge had
already expressed his opinion concerning his culpa-
bility. His fate, he claimed, had already been determined.

When the doors swung open to the journalists and
the public again on August 30, the crowd entering
the courtroom had already begun to thin out.
Akubzhanov then announced court adjourned for two
weeks until May 13.

When the trial resumed, Chikatilo announced
that in the interim while he was working on a novel,

he had suddenly remembered killing four more women. The only problem was that his recollection of their features, as well as the dates and locale of the murders, was suspiciously murky, in comparison to the brilliant memory he displayed while recounting all the other crimes. It seemed, in the long run, to be nothing more than a ploy to drag out the trial and buy himself some extra time. The logic behind it made perfect sense—more episodes would require further investigation, and more time for him.

Defense lawyer Khabibulin again moved that his client be subjected to a second psychiatric evaluation, and, to everyone's surprise, his sparring partner, public prosecutor Gerasimenko supported him. Gerasimenko was just as annoyed as the defense at the judge for effectively condemning the defendant while the trial was still in session. Akubzhanov and his lay assessors left the room to debate the merits of the motion. They returned a few minutes later and rejected it as groundless.

Khabibulin rose again from his seat in front of the cage, and announced that he rejected the composition of the court, which had called into question the mental state of his client and, therefore, was not fit to continue hearing the case. Chikatilo seconded his lawyer.

To the utter amazement of everyone, Gerasimenko also rejected the composition of the court, citing the fact that the defendant had already been prematurely judged in the press. He also pointed to procedural violations that had been committed by

Judge Akubzhanov. The judge, in his opinion, was not conducting himself properly—he was lecturing and insulting the defendant, and some of his statements led one to believe that the court's decision had already been made. Everyone was dumbfounded at the unexpected agreement between the prosecution and the defense.

The court again retired to the judge's chambers to confer. Naturally, it rejected the notion of removing itself—the whole idea was too farfetched. Instead, the judge called for the testimony of the witnesses to begin. More than four hundred were called, but only a few dozen actually showed up.

On May 18 a rumor began making the rounds that the "trial of the century" was a farce. The following day brought another sensation. One of the witnesses, O.A. Fomin, whose son was one of the victims charged to Chikatilo, proclaimed, "I petition for the removal of the prosecutor, Gerasimenko. Both the prosecution and the defense are making a mockery of this court. The prosecutor is concerned for Chikatilo's welfare, but who thought of us, the families, whose children he killed? If the prosecutor stays, I won't come back here anymore." Khabibulin voted against this proposal, while Chikatilo told them to figure it out on their own.

Gerasimenko replied to the man's charges that he understood the sentiments of the families, but that, in all respect, he had no intention of quitting the proceedings.

After yet another discussion with his assessors, Judge Akubzhanov informed the public that Fomin's request had been granted. Gerasimenko left.

The trial then had to be adjourned for a week. Someone had spilled mercury in the building—fingers pointed at the medical experts—and the building had to be cleared out until it could be declared free of poisonous gases. This interruption irritated everyone, especially the families of the victims and the witnesses who had been scheduled to give testimony on specific dates and wanted to get this thing over with quickly as possible. The first, maddening delay had been caused by the unprecedented removal of the prosecutor. His concern for the individual in the cage had angered witnesses and families to the point where, on one occasion, they began overturning the heavy benches and closing in on the defendant, shouting and threatening. Chikatilo was fortunate to have an armed cordon of guards posted around the perimeter of his cage.

The trial reopened one week later, amid much griping about the lack of a prosecutor and a host of other procedural violations. Judge Akubzhanov immediately adjourned it for another week. So far, he had not received any answer from Moscow to his telegrammed request to the Prosecutor General of Russia for a replacement for Gerasimenko. On June 2, the trial continued without a prosecutor. Even by Russian standards of jurisprudence, that seemed an outrageous breach of protocol.

Moscow's replacement for Gerasimenko had to cancel, citing unfamiliarity with the details of the case, and the second choice had already left on vacation. The next day two public prosecutors, Anatoly Ivanovich Zadorozhny and Aleksandr Borisovich Kuyumdzhi, were handpicked by Akubzhanov to fill the void left by Gerasimenko. It was at about this time of the trial that Chikatilo began ranting about the judge's ties to the "Assyrian mafia," for which he was issued a stern warning and told to sit down. In defiance of the judge's orders, Chikatilo remained on his feet, shouting something incomprehensible. Akubzhanov again warned the defendant that he would have him removed from the courtroom. From then on, each session would end in a shouting match between the judge and the defendant.

The defense wanted to know why the prosecution had two lawyers. The judge retired for a few moments to ponder the question, before claiming there was nothing illegal about it. Court was adjourned for another week, in order for the two new prosecutors to get acquainted with the 222 volumes of the case.

As this spectacle dragged out into the summer, fewer and fewer people attended. The only noteworthy incident during this period occurred when Chikatilo suddenly pulled his pants down in front of a startled public and began waving his penis at them. "Look at this useless thing," he cried. "What do you think I could do with that?"

On the morning following this outrage, Chikatilo again assumed his normal hunched and bent over position in his cage. When everyone had taken their seats after court had been called into session, Chikatilo remained standing. With one hand he pulled off his shirt with the Olympic rings motif— the only shirt he wore throughout the trial—and with the other he unbuttoned his pants, leaving him stark naked. After a moment of confusion, guards burst into the cage, pulled his pants up, shoved him out of the cage and literally threw him down the stairs. They returned a few moments later with a fully clothed and handcuffed defendant.

Chikatilo was not allowed to return to the courtroom until July 2. He would try again to expose himself before the public, a gesture that seemed carefully thought out and rehearsed in advance. Each time before he made the decision to drop his pants—even while handcuffed—he would survey the room and appraise his audience. The times when foreign journalists were present were obviously deemed more preferable.

His tactics gradually changed. Whereas in May he was still giving testimony and in June maintaining a silent stance, by July he had turned aggressive, using every opportunity to interrupt anyone who wanted to speak by raving about the judge being bought off by the Assyrian mafia, and about his autobiographical novel that would establish him as a literary genius. This was old stuff; what had changed in his tirades was that he would suddenly switch from Russian to

Ukrainian and demand that translators from Russian to Ukrainian and from Ukrainian to Abyssinian or Assyrian—a fresh dig at the judge—be brought in.

He demanded a new lawyer. With the two new prosecutors added to the judge and his assessors, he asserted that he was now one against five. He wanted a second attorney, too. He claimed that the Ukrainian nationalist movement, Rukh, had found one for him—a certain Stepan Romanovich Shevchenko. It was highly unlikely that such an attorney existed. The name was a hybrid of Stepan Romanovich, his alleged older and cannibalized brother, and Taras Shevchenko, the great nineteenth century Ukrainian poet.

All through this round of demands for a new attorney, the court displayed a tremendous amount of patience, even asking the defendant to give them the man's address so they could at least try and contact him. Chikatilo cursed the judge with a stream of invectives, even though this kind of language had supposedly made him blush in the past. He would not let the judge get a word in edgewise. Finally, after receiving about his tenth warning, Chikatilo was forcibly removed from the room. As he was led out of the cage, he launched into a Ukrainian folk song.

In addition to the demands described above, Chikatilo insisted that the judge's secretary, Yelena Khramova, be replaced by a man, claiming that her presence in the room was inciting his lust. He also claimed he was pregnant, and that the guards were hitting him in his swollen belly with their clubs.

* * *

On July 3, Dr. Bukhanovsky was finally called to the trial, but only in the capacity of witness. For three hours he patiently answered the questions posed to him by the judge, the prosecution and the defense. Judge Akubzhanov eventually caved in to the numerous demands for a second medical opinion.

Andrei Tkachenko and Inna Ushakova, both of whom had signed the first opinion a year ago, were summoned to Rostov from the Serbsky Institute. So were two other specialists, including Ivan Bakumenko, the leading psychiatrist in the Rostov province and head of the local commission which had briefly examined the defendant in May.

After spending one whole day studying all the materials of the case, reading the descriptions of the defendant made by his various cellmates, and interviewing the defendant himself, the commission reported its conclusion: Chikatilo was competent to stand trial. He had obviously been faking his complaints of troubled sleep and headaches, based on his cellmates' reports of his healthy appetite. He would even ask them to share their food with him. They had also reported that he was a sound sleeper, though he might wake upon occasion in the middle of the night to have a snack before falling instantly back to sleep.

He was unfailingly polite and sociable with his cellmates, and sound in his judgments. In addition, he showed consistency in his written statements by seriously responding to any questions concerning his case and his health. His strange behavior in the courtroom, the commission concluded, was nothing more than a calculated attempt for acquittal on grounds of insanity.

As far as his sexual dysfunction was concerned, one of the experts considered it to be a rather widespread phenomenon. Many other men suffered from similar disorders, but this did not lead them to commit shocking crimes.

Even after their opinion had been rendered, there still remained a sense of incompleteness and inconclusiveness. Perhaps defense lawyer Khabibulin had been correct in wondering aloud whether or not, for the sake of objectivity, a different group of experts from institutes other than the Serbsky should have been consulted.

It was now the middle of July; the trial was nearing its end. Interest had begun to fade. At first, newspapers had satisfied the public's curiosity for sensational details, but now they limited themselves to brief reports. Boredom reigned in the courtroom. A daily pattern had been established: the judge continued to read the indictment in a monotone while Chikatilo was constantly being evicted from the room for scandalous behavior.

The pleading of both sides began on August 10. As he was being forcibly shoved out of his cage for the umpteenth time, Chikatilo cried out in Ukrainian, "Long live free Ukraine!"

The prosecution went first. With Zadorozhny and Kuyumdzhi dividing the episodes of the indictment between them, they made it perfectly clear to the public that they were absolutely convinced of the defendant's guilt, citing the testimony of witnesses, the conclusion of the medical experts, and Chikatilo's own confessions. They stated that the defendant's actions should be properly construed in accordance with Article 102 of the Criminal Code of the Russian Federation as premeditated, and especially cruel, murder. At the end of his summation, Kuyumdzhi said that there was only one word that could be used to characterize the defendant, and that word was "murderer." The prosecution asked for capital punishment.

The next day was Marat Khabibulin's turn to present the case for the defense. He had sat throughout the trial in one of the most conspicuous places—right in front of the defendant's cage—and had been photographed by dozens of photojournalists and news agencies. Despite this, he managed to maintain a low profile while simultaneously conveying the impression of someone who had entered this courtroom by mistake, or at least of someone who looked out of place. In fact, he was not here to defend Chikatilo of his own volition, but had been appointed by the court. At one point he openly admitted that his client was no prize.

There was no chance of winning this case. Public opinion was already made up. During the trial, Khabibulin sat in his seat, emotionless, with a far-away look in his eyes. Up to this point he had done everything he possibly could for his client. After each session, he had visited Chikatilo in his jail cell and tried to dissuade him from any more outbursts, as they were only working against him. It was not his fault if his client did not heed his advice. He even had the sympathy of the families of the victims, who realized he was only doing his job.

His speech for the defense was reported in all the newspapers. In short, his argument boiled down to the following: not a single count against the defendant had been conclusively proven by either the investigation or the court, as there had not been a single witness who had seen the defendant allegedly commit his crimes. All the charges thus far had been based solely on the defendant's confession; there was not a single bit of material evidence irrefutably linking Chikatilo with the crimes, including the twenty-three knives which may or may not have been used as murder weapons. The psychiatric expertise could not be considered objective and independent, insofar as the institute where the experts worked had already proven itself to the whole world on numerous occasions to be a pawn of the government. He begged the court, therefore, to acquit his client.

Chikatilo was returned to the cage after his lawyer's speech, and asked if he had any final words he wanted to add in his defense. He refused, preferring to sit quietly in his cage and staring off into the distance.

The judge announced a two-month recess for the writing of the sentence. All had risen from their seats to go when Vadim Kulevatsky, brother of one of the victims and mentioned earlier as the only immediate family member to attend every single session of the trial, suddenly moved toward the cage and heaved a small, dark object at Chikatilo from a distance of less than six feet. There was the sound of a mute blow as the object, an iron rod about three inches long, struck a wall behind Chikatilo's ear. Had it struck him in the temple, there might not have been a defendant to sentence. Instead, it came off as a clumsy, theatrical, and naive assassination attempt. But for many people, the fact that Chikatilo was still alive at all was a source of constant amazement.

Public opinion in Russia had never much subscribed to the theory of presumption of innocence. One of the tabloid newspapers had already reported, in June 1992, that the famous "Rostov case" had ended with the death sentence. A more respectable newspaper, *Komsomolskaya Pravda*, wrote not long thereafter that, naturally, Chikatilo would be shot and that he was perfectly aware of this himself. In an article entitled "Vampire for Sale," the paper *Moscow News* reported that Chikatilo should not be executed, but sold to the Japanese who supposedly were prepared to buy him in order to study his brain. This idea was further elaborated upon by suggesting that he be traded to the Japanese in exchange for the Kurile Islands, a constant bone of contention

between the two countries since the end of World
War II.

★ ★ ★

The two months had passed and on October 14, the
public once again assembled in courtroom number
five. This time the room was filled to overflowing. To
make up for the previously less than desirable
acoustics, the room was now equipped with micro-
phones and amplifiers.

The defendant, who had visibly aged during this
last break in the trial, was pushed back into his cage.
Just as in the first days of the trial, flashbulbs popped,
cameras shuttered and whirred, videocameras
hummed. Just as before, the mothers of dead children
screamed, "Let us at him, we'll give him our own
verdict!" and "Where were the police earlier?"
Chikatilo sat turned to the side, smiling.

The judge and the two assessors entered the room.
All stood and remained standing until the verdict had
been read. Only the families of the victims were
allowed to take their seats. In a loud voice, Judge
Akubzhanov began to read the long and handwritten
verdict, but as soon as he began another voice, flat
and monotonous, issued from the cage. This duet
lasted for a few minutes until the defendant was
ordered out of the room. Because he was obligated to
hear the sentence, Chikatilo was allowed back in
from time to time, but he would just as quickly spew
his usual nonsense about free Ukraine, his pregnancy,
barricades, the Assyrian mafia and partisan fighters.

The judge read out in detail all the charges against Chikatilo for each crime uncovered by the investigation. Only one charge—for the murder of Laura Sarkisyan—was dropped for insufficient evidence. The defendant had not been able to positively identify the victim from photographs, and the circumstantial evidence had been weak as well.

During one of the times he was allowed back into the courtroom, Chikatilo called out that he had a petition to make to the court, but Akubzhanov cut him off sharply. "Too late! There's not going to be any petitions today. Today you get the verdict!" In reply, Chikatilo shouted, "Crook! I haven't confessed to anything!"

October 15, 1992 was the last day of the "trial of the century." The longer Akubzhanov read out the counts against the defendant, the more the room filled with tension. Many people succumbed to the gory details and fainted. Others, growing ever more impatient, stood on the benches to get a better look at the judge.

The defendant was brought up to his cage and sent back down again, screaming, "I'm an honest Ukrainian woman! You didn't give me the first word, or the last word, either. And I didn't steal any linoleum. I confessed to it under torture and the influence of drugs."

The judge was nearing the conclusion of the sentence. Chikatilo was back in his cage—he had to be present for the final pronouncement.

He was up to his tricks of speaking in tandem with the judge, trying to disrupt him, when the verdict came down: the guilt for the murder of fifty-two people had been proven; the court considered the defendant responsible for his actions; and, in consideration of the defendant's monstrous actions, the court sentenced him to death.

The room erupted in shouts of approval and applause. Through the din one voice could be heard, yelling "Fraud! I'm not going to listen to your lies!" Chikatilo was removed for the last time.

Akubzhanov then turned to reading out the criminal codes of Russia, Ukraine and Uzbekistan, the republics in which the crimes had been committed, and the punishment stipulated by each for rape and premeditated murder: capital punishment, capital punishment, fifteen years incarceration, capital punishment...

For the last time, Judge Akubzhanov ordered Chikatilo returned to his cage for their final exchange:

Akubzhanov: Chikatilo, this court has sentenced you to death. Do you understand the nature of the sentence?

Chikatilo: Crook!

Akubzhanov: I repeat, do you understand the sentence?

Chikatilo: Freedom for Russia and Ukraine! Crook!

At a press conference afterwards, Akubzhanov noted that he deliberately never uttered the words "death by shooting," because, in his opinion, that would not be enough for the defendant. He also said that Chikatilo would definitely appeal the sentence— in all his fourteen years as a judge every single one of his decisions had been appealed. That same evening Chikatilo was removed from the KGB isolation cell in the basement of the Rostov Department of Internal Affairs, since renamed the Department of Security, and taken to another isolation cell in Novocherkassk where he now sits on death row.

There are members of the legal profession in Russia who believe there are sufficient grounds for appealing the verdict. But if the Supreme Court upholds Akubzhanov's decision, which seems a foregone conclusion, the accused and his lawyer can appeal to the president of Russia for clemency. At the moment, a special committee has been empowered to address the issue of clemency. Its members are neither legal professionals nor administrators, but average working people. It is said that the commission can present its opinion to President Boris Yeltsin at the end of 1993.

It is also said that President Yeltsin is a stern individual and not given to sentiment.